Carving
on Turning

Chris Pye

Guild of Master Craftsman Publications Ltd

Guild of Master Craftsman Publications Ltd

First published 1995 by
Guild of Master Craftsman Publications Ltd
166 High Street, Lewes
East Sussex BN7 1XU

© Christopher J. Pye, 1995,
Reprinted 2000

Line drawings, photographs and cover
photography © Christopher J. Pye 1995

ISBN 0 946819 88 2

Designed by Martin Lovelock

Set in Garamond, printed on fineblade

Origination supervised by MRM Graphics

Printed in Hong Kong by H & Y Printing Ltd

For my son Daniel

Contents

Acknowledgements

I would like to thank all those who have helped me with this book, singling out five people in particular for my especial thanks:

Don White, a solid and talented woodturner, for help and encouragement in the past, and for the use of the bowl he turned – which appears, lettered, in Chapter 6; Nick Hough, editor of *Woodturning* magazine, for his quiet confidence and support while I was writing the original series of articles on which this book is based; Liz Inman, my editor, for her enthusiasm, always working so wholeheartedly towards the best result; Jonathan Ingoldby for his perceptive copy editing and thoughtful approach; and Karin Vogel, my wife, for her creative contribution to both the projects and my well-being.

Introduction

CHAPTER 1

This book has arisen from the ashes of a series of 14 articles which I wrote for *Woodturning* magazine, starting in issue 15. I wanted to gather the material together, add new information, and present it as a whole. The series itself came about as a response to requests from turners to show them something about carving; some techniques with which they could experiment and extend the scope of their work.

The vast majority of turners today turn as a secondary occupation; there are very few who make a living from it, although many sell items to supplement their income. Most are content with the enjoyment that comes from a craft which allows them to produce beautiful and functional objects at a fairly early stage, yet which has endless avenues to explore and skills to perfect.

This exploration is evident in the ever extending boundaries of turning. Increasingly, it involves a crossing of traditional limits, a taking in of other materials such as resins, stone or metal, the use of finishes such as burning or staining, or crafts like silversmithing or woodcarving. Sometimes I have a sense that this is overdone, and that turners are locked into the same 'tyranny of the new' as art as a whole seems to be, where in order to make a name for yourself you have to be different, *somehow*. Nevertheless, some of the pieces being produced today are quite extraordinary, and show how human beings can take their skills from many sources in the hunt to trap their inspiration.

In *Woodturning* magazine, right from its inception, many fine examples of turned work can be found which have been enhanced by shaping or carving. These range from simple, decorative tool marks, to quite elaborate undertakings which have in them more carving and shaping than turning. Carving is increasingly becoming one of those adventurous departures, helping a turner to break free of lathe restraints into other dimensions. This book is offered in the hope that the techniques and information within will gradually help turners to develop their explorations.

I have been asked by turners about books on carving, and as far as

I am aware there is nothing published which combines turning and carving as it is covered in my original series of magazine articles, or in this book. But you will find lots of useful ideas and techniques if you care to look around. The Stobart Davies' catalogue of woodworking books lists almost everything in print, along with a brief description of each book and is a good starting point. However, I would suggest that you look at any book first, rather than buying unseen through the mail. Carving books are wide and varied in content and approach and you may end up with one about carving driftwood sculpture when all you wanted was to texture the surface of your goblets. If you have the patience, getting your local library to order a book first is a good idea. A list of titles I personally recommend can be found in the bibliography.

CARVING AND TURNING

I started by carving wood before I learned to turn it, and I only started turning wood for money, so it was important to reach a high standard of efficiency and skill quickly. To begin with I applied turning skills to separate items from those which I was carving, making whatever customers wanted: furniture legs by the hundred, bowls and boxes. But after a while I found myself combining the two crafts for particular work, and having to find new approaches. The fact that I have this background 'in the trade' is probably the reason for the projects in this book being fairly traditional or familiar. My aim is to introduce simple, graspable ideas and methods of working, starting at the beginning, and then leave the rest to you.

I think I found turning easy because of my background in carving. I would guess it is always easier this way – rather than for a turner to become a carver. As I note later, each craft has a different speed of work, which suits what seem to be basic differences in temperament between turners and carvers. For example, I have always been encouraged on a cold morning by getting straight away into the lathe's friendly sense of energy and rhythm; whereas on the carving bench, where tools are picked up one by one, nothing happens unless I make it happen and picking up rhythm can be more difficult.

I have been asked many times, is carving more difficult than turning? I have to lay my cards on the table here and say yes, I think it is. Having said that, I am not lessening turning, or in any way saying that turning is easy, or anything other than a fulfilling and absorbing craft. I also would be among the first to agree that comparisons are odious. My response comes from my teaching experience: someone new to turning could expect to be sufficiently competent to make simple bowls quite soon, often within hours. The equivalent level of competence in carving would take far longer to reach: weeks, perhaps months. Having said this, a great deal depends on aptitude and, above all, motivation.

It must be remembered that carving can be an extremely wide, elaborate and demanding three-dimensional skill, seen taken to its limits in, say, the 11-metre high altars (retables) of the southern German Tilman Riemenschneider. It is a skill that in its own right can occupy a lifetime. But this is not to say that turners cannot dip into the craft, taking away some basic skills to add to those they already have and through this combination of skills create satisfying objects of great beauty.

The application of carving disciplines to woodturning has a long history – you only have to look at furniture such as four-poster beds for an example (see Fig 1.1). This sort of work would have been done by two separate tradesmen: a turner and a carver. There is no such thing as carving purely for turning – a sort of 'tarving' or 'curning'. There is woodcarving, and woodturning, and you can mix them. If you can carve decent letters on to the rim of a bowl or other turned work, you can carve them on to anything (see Fig 1.2).

All crafts have their particular tools and methods of working, to be learned, enjoyed and used. Woodcarving is no exception. In this book I repeat myself at various points. I make no apologies for this, as some ideas or methods of working are so important that they need to be repeated until they become second nature.

FIG 1.1 A TRADITIONAL APPLICATION OF CARVING TO TURNING: A FOUR-POSTER BEDPOST.

FIG 1.2 LETTERING ON TO A BOWL BY DON WHITE.

LEARNING TO CARVE

Newcomers often ask: how long does it take to become a competent carver? Such a difficult question, but one that it seems so reasonable to ask. My answer is always that so much depends on who *you* are; your ability and motivation, and the time you have to practise. It also depends on how we assess this thing called 'competence', or what makes a 'good' carving, and on what level of carving we are talking about; what goals you will set yourself, and at what level you will be happy. At the end of the day competence may simply mean being able to make what you have in your mind's eye – even if you only want to carve in a limited fashion to a limited but particular end. Not necessarily 'efficient' – which is what I have to be when carving to a cost – but achieving your aims, which can include just having fun.

I have sometimes felt that turners are a bit overawed by carving, especially on the grand scale. But – and this may sound prosaic – there are only two things you need to do if you want to learn how to carve: you need to start, somewhere, and then continue. You will eventually discover, from others or by trial and error, what you need to know. The skills are there for anyone who wants to learn, enjoys the sense of exploration, and is motivated to keep going. I hope it is helpful to lay this out in a little more detail.

FIG 1.3 A DETAIL OF THE KOI CARP POST WHICH SUPPORTS A CEILING BEAM IN A WILTSHIRE KITCHEN. THE POST IS ONE PIECE OF OAK, 7 FEET LONG (2.1M) AND 7IN (178MM) IN DIAMETER. ONLY THE TURNING IS SANDED. THE FISH HEAD SHOWS THE TOOLS CUTS AND GOUGE MARKS WHICH FORM THE SCALES. STRONG GRAIN WOULD OBSCURE THESE DETAILS.

- **Making a start**

  Putting it simply, you've got to get in there and have a go, rather than just thinking about it.

- **Learn as you go**

  Cultivate an attitude of learning – this is very important. Learn from what you have done, both the successes and the mistakes. There is no end to learning. It also helps to keep interest, challenge and opportunity alive.

- **Continuing to work at it**

  This means keeping going. It may be a bit simplistic to say that 'practice makes perfect' as there is definitely such a thing as natural flair or ability. But regular practice really helps progress whatever it is you want to learn. My experience of students is that those who put in a bit of effort in between sessions progress far more quickly than those who don't.

- **Pay attention to the carving tools**

  Respect them, look after them, learn to sharpen them properly and keep them sharp. Sharpening is never wasted time. In carving, this emphasis on the tools is an extremely important idea to grasp.

- **Enjoy your carving**

  A final, but perhaps most important, point. Enjoy your exploration into a new craft, the way it can widen the range of what you make, and open your eyes to a world of decoration and sculpture that you will understand as only someone who has tried it can understand.

This is also exactly the kind of advice I would give to someone learning turning. So perhaps another approach is to ask yourself how you became a competent turner and apply the same method. Turners already have many skills, of hand and eye, which are transferable to carving; they have a head start over many who later succeed in the craft of carving but who come to it with nothing.

CARVING AND SHAPING

I find it helpful to differentiate between *carving* and *shaping*. Carving involves the traditional trade tools and methods. The wood itself is only a support for the light and shadow of forms and details created by the carving cuts themselves (see Fig 1.3). This is why most carved work, past and present, is executed in bland woods like lime, beech, mahogany and oak. Strong grain would camouflage or confuse the carving – imagine letters cut in zebrawood! The carving on furniture to be French-polished may be sanded but, by and large, good carving can be left straight from the chisel.

Shaping is where the grain and figuring of the wood are given a place of at least equal prominence to the form of a piece (see Fig 1.4). It is a much more recent phenomenon and frequently exhibits itself in sculpture. There is a strong element, in this sense, of shaping wood in turning, where the inherent qualities of the wood are particularly sought. A 'shaper', then, may never use a carving tool, preferring rasps, files, sandpaper and the high speed flexible drives with burrs and cutters which are becoming more popular.

This is not to say that carving tools are not used to shape, or that carvers never use rasps, or that one is 'better' than the other; they are both means to ends. Distinguishing carving and shaping in this way will help make your approach to a piece of work clearer in your mind, by seeing the needs of the design balanced between wood and method.

In this book I primarily address the more complicated aspects of carving, as it is my experience that more people need help in this area. However, there will be opportunities for discussing shaping as well.

ASSUMPTIONS ABOUT THE READER

I have assumed the reader to have at least a basic understanding and competence in woodturning, both between centres and in faceplate work.

Although I have included some notes on what I think makes a 'good' turning, I intend to describe only salient turning points in any project as they arise. I will assume no experience with carving and start at the beginning, with the necessary tools and equipment.

LAYOUT OF THE BOOK

Chapters 2 and 3 lay some necessary groundwork. Subsequent chapters contain projects which are arranged to build up a range of useful carving techniques, applicable to other contexts. Questions and answers that appeared in the article series have been incorporated into the body of material presented here.

Chapter 2, Turning, while making the assumption about an ability to turn on the part of the reader, is a bit of a catch-all for

information I think specifically relevant to the contents of this book.

In Chapter 3, Carving, I conduct a brief guided tour around the various shapes of woodcarving tools, with some notes on what they can do, and then look at what is needed to sharpen them. As the nature and size of this book put a limit on the information that, ideally, I would like to have included I must mention another book, *Woodcarving Tools, Materials and Equipment* (see bibliography for details) which I wrote as a sort of background, almost reference, manual for woodcarvers, or indeed anyone wanting to use carving tools at all. It goes into far greater depth about the tools, their sharpening and use, holding devices, wood and so on and will be very useful for anyone interested in the application of woodcarving to turning, backing up the information given in these pages.

There is a rough plan of increasing complexity to the following sequence of chapters, which are project orientated. I proceed, not always in a straight line, from the making of simple cuts, marks and textured surfaces, through low and high relief, to work in the round, taking in some lettering on the way. Three chapters relate to aspects of furniture work, a field in which many turners are already involved.

FIG 1.4 THE LOTUS SHRINE IN THE MANCHESTER BUDDHIST CENTRE IS 36IN (914MM) IN DIAMETER AT THE MAXIMUM WIDTH OF THE OUTSIDE FLOWER. THERE ARE TWO 'FLOWERS' AND A CENTRE DISC. THE FLOWERS WERE MADE LIKE NORMAL BOWLS OR PLATTERS ON A FACEPLATE, BUT ON A HUGE PATTERNMAKER'S LATHE. ONE BOWL WAS MADE TO FIT INSIDE THE OTHER, AND BOTH WERE TURNED TO A PRECONCEIVED PROFILE MORE THAN $\frac{1}{2}$IN (13MM) THICK. THESE BOWLS WERE THEN CARVED WITH SEPARATE LEAVES, THE SURFACES OF WHICH WERE MODELLED. THE UNDERSIDE REFLECTED THE SHAPES ON THE TOPSIDE. THE DISC ITSELF IS MAPLE, BLEACHED AND WHITE WAXED. BESIDES SHARING A SYMBOLIC SIGNIFICANCE WITH THE SHRINE AS A WHOLE THE DISC SERVES TO HIDE THE STEEL STUDDING HOLDING THE WHOLE PIECE TOGETHER.

Specific projects that you have in mind and specific technical problems can usually be dealt with by adapting the basic techniques, relaxing, and just having a go. If this risks ruining a piece of valuable turning, should you fail to get it right, the best advice is to do a sample first.

If you follow the course of the book – if only by reading it – you should have begun to get an impression of how woodcarving is at once both logical and simple, and yet very wide in its scope and possibilities. I have only been able to cover a small fraction of what a woodcarver may do – what *you* as carvers may do – and that mostly along more traditional lines.

I will finish by wishing you well with your exploration of carving, and hope that you find within this book some skills and effects that will be useful to you in your work, and which will help increase your satisfaction in what you do.

Turning

CHAPTER 2

I said in the previous chapter that I would assume readers of this book to have a reasonable knowledge of turning. I felt that the majority would be interested in adding carving techniques to their existing skills to see whether there was a possibility of extending the scope of their current work.

However, I still want to look a little closer at turning, for the simple reason that the quality of the final product will depend both on the initial turning as well as the secondary carving – and it is usually this way round – turning first, then carving. I cannot think of a piece which I carved first and then put back on the lathe – although this may just be my particular way of working. Sometimes a piece has a lot of turning and the carving is a mere flourish. Elsewhere the opposite is true and turning takes a secondary role. On yet other occasions there is a balance between the two. If you look at the projects in this book you will see this variable balance. However, in every case, whatever the weighting between turning and carving, good turning is still needed to get the best overall result.

There is insufficient room in this book to go into the technical aspects of woodturning in any detail. There are many excellent books, magazines and courses about turning on the market, and I

FIG 2.1 TURNING TOOLS, COMPARED WITH THOSE USED FOR CARVING, ARE RELATIVELY SIMPLE. THEY STILL NEED TO BE CORRECTLY SHARPENED AND MANIPULATED FOR THE BEST RESULT.

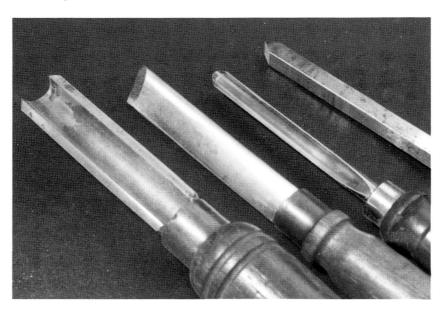

have made some book and magazine suggestions in the bibliography. In this chapter I will look at some of the ways turning and carving work together: what contributes, in my view, to a 'good' piece of turning; some features and modifications of the lathe that I find of great use, such as indexing plates; wood and grain and the different needs and approaches required between the turner and carver; and finally a little bit about finishing.

WAYS IN WHICH TURNING AND CARVING WORK TOGETHER

When turning and carving appear on the same workpiece, each contributing to the final appearance, there must be a dynamic between the two. They must be working together, even if the design of the piece means that they are deliberately working *against* each other.

As I have said, most of the time turning is completed first in the process of making a turned and carved object. As I am turning the wood I will have the subsequent carving in mind, and will be referring in my mind to the carving at all times and the way the turning is affecting it.

There follows a list of some of the ways in which turning and carving work or function together. It is by no means exclusive but may help to bring awareness to what is happening when you design a piece. Also, bear in mind that these functions may overlap and a piece may have several factors operating simultaneously, as illustrated by several of the projects later in the book. In some of the projects I have made a point of discussing further the design features that were in my mind.

- **The turning may support the carving (e.g. the milking stool and frog box projects)**
  Essentially the turned part of the work is 'showing off' the carving – displaying it. In a way this is similar to a piece of music where the orchestra plays rather mutely to support a solo instrument. Without the well-played background rhythms and context the solo playing would be the poorer. By analogy turning which supports carving in this muted but crucial way must still be done well.

- **The turning may be functional in its own right (e.g. the bedpost and milking stool projects)**
  In other words, if the turning is a box, then the lid should open

and fit as properly as if the carving were absent. Similarly, a stool is something to sit on, so the legs must be strong enough for the stool to be used. This is a point that is independent of carving and applies to turned work as a whole.

- **The turning may balance, or contrast with, the carving (e.g. the lettered bowl project)**
  In the bowl there is central space which allows the letters to stand out. The lettering also follows the rim, and in reading the carved text the viewer becomes aware of the turned nature of the piece. Another example would be the way in which, quite often, simple turning contrasts with more complicated carving.

- **The turning and carving may be equally important (e.g. the pestle and mortar project)**
  When you see such a balanced piece your eye is moving between the carved and turned elements all the time with neither being dominant. This is especially true of shaped work and textured surfaces.

- **The turning creates the profile for the carving (e.g. the patera, gadroons and frog box projects)**
  In effect the turner does some of the preliminary work of the carver, and indeed there are plenty of carvers who, not turning wood, will approach a turner with a profile. Sometimes, as with the pestle and mortar, the lathe cannot help but show its axial nature and leave a profile in places other than those which were intended.

'GOOD' TURNING

Whether a piece of turning is 'good' or 'bad' is one of those value judgements which we all make but perhaps don't share with others. Perhaps the terms 'good' or 'bad' are themselves not very helpful, but I'm still going to use them for the sake of simplicity.

It is very important that you try your best to turn wood as well as possible – not only will your turned work be a foil for the carving, but it will be present in its own right. Always strive for excellence in your craft, whether turning or carving.

I have assembled a few guidelines as to what I think makes a good piece of turning. I will not try to justify what follows – I don't think I am being controversial. I hope that by bearing these points in mind you will improve the standard of your turning.

Design

Designing means both originating a scheme, project or piece of work and also laying it out, preparing it and thinking through the arrangement of its parts. It surprises me how many turners design on the hoof, going straight into the wood without much preconception of what they wish to achieve. This is fine if you don't mind repeating the process until you get it right, but as often as not the end product demonstrates the need for thinking a piece of work through before you begin, which of course applies to carving as well.

It's a good exercise to work out as much as you can before committing an idea to a fixed form; it is far easier to adjust things on paper than after they have been cut in to the wood. You will find that primary, secondary and tertiary masses or forms have their own effects and mutual tensions; that lines guide the eye and there are balances to be struck between details and space, between various proportions, and so on.

Good turning always pays attention to the design, the plan of the thing, the elements and how they compound into a whole; its structure and how the piece works three-dimensionally. You can always sense this in a good piece of turning.

Craftsmanship

Whatever the design, it must be executed competently; that is, clearly following the intentions of the designer. So, for example,

FIG 2.2 IN BOTH TURNING AND CARVING THE CLARITY AND SENSITIVITY OF THE PROFILE IS VERY IMPORTANT IN THE OVERALL IMPRESSION OF A PIECE.

curved lines should have a definite and clean shape, 'flats' should be avoided on convex surfaces and concave surfaces should have no additional ridges or grooves. Where fillets mark changes in direction they should be cut neatly without interrupting the flow of the curves. Where your intention is to have a smooth surface then this is what you should produce, without torn grain or ridges.

With regard to sanding, if you are not careful sanding tends to round over the crisp shapes and lines of a turning and gives it a boiled sweet appearance. Cut a smooth, crisp, exact surface first so that it needs hardly any sanding, then sand. Spindles should never be scraped.

Remember that both turnings and carvings are handled and touched. I use a sense of touch, even closing my eyes when it is safe, to feel the surface of what I make. It's a good way to get a sense of pure form, independent of surface figuring which may confuse matters.

SOME FEATURES AND MODIFICATIONS TO THE LATHE

The features of your lathe depend a bit on how much you paid for it. Most of the turning in this book is very basic and involves simple tools, and equipment that most lathes will have, whatever their size and cost. However, to carve work efficiently, I have found three features very useful: an ability to lock the lathe mandrel, an indexing plate and a carving tool table. I have never regretted the time spent acquiring these features. The first two are not necessarily included

FIG 2.4

FIG 2.5

FIG 2.4 To control a V tool, and chase smooth, exact lines like these, work must be held completely stationary, either on the lathe or on the bench.

FIG 2.5 A quick temporary method for preventing the mandrel of a lathe turning. Only really suitable for light work as the wedge is not a strong locking system.

on even the most expensive lathes, and the latter is tricky to place on lathes with rounded ways. In addition, special means of supporting work may be necessary.

Locking devices

The Harrison Graduate I use has a spanner which fits across the mandrel, holding it while faceplates and chucks are unscrewed. The spanner is hand-held and there is a considerable degree of movement possible within the pulley housing where the spanner is offered. This is fine for its purpose (unscrewing faceplates) but not for carving. When you are carving wood it is imperative that the wood is fixed and stays still if you are going to maintain control in a safe manner (see Fig 2.4). This also applies when the workpiece is supported away from the lathe and on a bench for carving. Another

FIG 2.6 Using a faceplate on the outboard spindle and the outboard toolrest holder, a simple but strong lock can be given to the mandrel.

FIG 2.7 Close-up of Fig 2.6: the work can be easily repositioned.

FIG 2.6

FIG 2.7

FIG 2.8

FIG 2.9

requirement is that the wood needs to be locked in the position in which you want it.

All that may be necessary to achieve this position locking, as with the Harrison, is a wedge between the mandrel and the pulley housing, gently but firmly preventing the mandrel rotating (see Fig 2.5). When the mandrel is locked, which will be when you want to start carving, the lathe should be isolated to remove any danger of it being accidentally switched on. Another simple idea is to use the outboard spindle (see Fig 2.6). To lock the mandrel on your own lathe may need a little more ingenuity. Whatever you use try and make it simple; you want to be able to make position adjustments as easily and quickly as possible (see Fig 2.7).

Indexing plates

This is not a feature of my Harrison lathe but is now much commoner on newer designs. Again some resourcefulness may be needed, and when in use the lathe should be isolated.

Usually, if you are using the indexing plate the mandrel is secure enough not to need a locking device as well (see Figs 2.8 and 2.9). If you are considering fairly violent work, using a mallet, then the workpiece should come off the lathe and on to the bench to prevent the possibility of damaging either the indexing plate, mandrel or bearings.

You will see the use of the indexing plate to divide up work before carving on many occasions in this book. If you only want to make a

FIG 2.8 ON MY LARGER LATHE I HAVE ADDED THIS LOCKING AND INDEXING PLATE THROUGH WHICH THE DRIVE CENTRE CONTINUES TO FUNCTION. OTHER PLATES, WITH DIFFERENT NUMBERS OF HOLES, CAN BE FIXED TO THE INNER PLATE, WHICH IS NOTHING LESS THAN A THICK FACEPLATE.

FIG 2.9 BACK VIEW OF FIG 2.8: THE PIN IS KEPT IN THE HOLE IN THE INDEXING PLATE BY THE SPRING; WHEN RETRACTED THE PLATE CAN BE ROTATED TO THE NEXT POINT. THE PIN CAN BE LOCKED FURTHER AWAY FROM THE PLATE BY THE KNOB.

FIG 2.10

FIG 2.11

FIG 2.10 A QUICKLY MADE INDEXING
PLATE WHICH USES AN OUTBOARD
FACEPLATE, TOOLREST HOLDER AND A
SMALL BOLT.

FIG 2.11 CLOSE-UP OF FIG 2.10: YOU
STILL NEED TO BE ACCURATE IN THE
INITIAL MARKING AND ASSEMBLY OF
THE INDEXING PLATE TO GET THE
BEST RESULTS, BUT THE TIME IS WELL
SPENT.

few objects then you can divide easily enough with masking tape wrapped round the work and folded. If you have an outboard spindle on your lathe then it may be easiest to use an outboard faceplate and tool rest as part of the set up (see Figs 2.10 and 2.11).

Carving tool table

When you are carving you need somewhere convenient to lay tools down safely and accessibly. A simple board clamped to the bed of the lathe will do the job, optionally with a fence around the edge to stop your tools accidentally rolling on to the floor (see Fig 2.12). In the projects you will see this in use almost every time the lathe is used to support the work.

FIG 2.12 A TOOL TABLE KEEPS
CARVING TOOLS AND OTHER BITS AND
PIECES SAFE WHILE CARVING IS
PROCEEDING ON THE LATHE ABOVE.

FIG 2.13 A SUPPORTING SADDLE FOR
SPINDLES. THE METAL BRACKET
WHICH FITS INTO THE TOOLREST
HOLDER I HAD MADE BY A LOCAL
METALWORKER.

Supporting work

In both turning and carving, as wood becomes thinner it becomes more flexible and hence more vulnerable. Sometimes it needs more support than can be given by your hands alone. An example is barley-twisted and other similarly carved spindles; here a simple trough supported by the tool rest enables you to work with far more confidence (see Fig 2.13).

All woods are potentially carvable – just as they are potentially turnable. And as with turning, the wood needs to be matched to the design.

Carving is essentially about creating light and shadow. An example of mistaken wood use would be to support carved lettering with a figured wood. In such a case the figuring effectively camouflages or obscures what is meant to be seen clearly. On the other hand there are many occasions where figuring can be used to enhance carving, especially in the case of shaped forms.

Another mistake is to use a coarse or open grained wood for fine detailed carving, where a tight grain is needed.

I would suggest starting with a mild, 'carver friendly' timber such as limewood or a fruit wood. Practise using the tools a little before committing your cuts to valuable turnings or wood.

Even when you are becoming proficient at carving it may be a good idea to practise your intended design first, especially when the turned part of a project has itself taken a lot of time and effort. As Pooh Bear found, what seems a Good Idea in your head is not necessarily such a good one when you say it out loud – or carve it.

WOODS FOR CARVING

Very common questions I get from turners concern dealing with grain. The grain strikes them as far more complicated and problematic when carving wood than when turning it.

The principles of working grain – that is, the fibres of the wood – are the same in all woodcrafts. It just seems more complicated when carving because you are working from all directions and changing direction all the time. The secret is that, as you carve, you must be sensitive to what is happening at the moment the wood is cut, reacting immediately and reversing the direction when you find the grain tearing. With properly sharpened carving tools you can happily work across the grain, which considerably lessens the problem. You can even carve against the grain when there is no alternative.

FINISHING
There is nothing special that carvers do to finish their work that turners do not do. Indeed, woodturning is richer in its repertoire of finishing techniques than carving, so there are no secrets for the turner here.

Finish to protect and enhance, revealing the beauty of the work through such qualities as clarity of form and line, surface texture or figuring, and the colour of the wood itself. Remember that most finishes will reveal torn fibres and scratches more than leaving the wood in the white. If you have used razor-sharp carving tools (as you should), they will leave facets that are burnished by the bevel of the tool, which can be oiled and waxed with no further work. If your tools are rough they will leave scratch marks and torn grain which will be immediately evident.

Carving

For almost all my turned work, which covers a range of sizes from enormous newel posts to small boxes, I use about ten turning tools: two sizes of roughing gouges, three spindle gouges, three skews and two parting chisels. Throw in the odd scraper for the bottom of the box and that's it. Day in, day out, these tools are the ones I need and use. On some work I may use only one of them. The same applies to the majority of turners. A quick touch to the grinding wheel when the edges of the chosen tool become dull and back to work. Because turning tools are made of high speed steel (HSS), a little blueing from over-eager grinding makes no difference to their cutting properties or their ability to hold a sharp edge.

Carving is a different matter. The number of tools I need is much larger, and their shapes are more elaborate. For a simple piece of work I might only use one or two chisels or gouges, but where the work is more complicated, several dozen may be needed to deal with the problems and complications of the form. Over the years, through taking on a wide variety and size of carving work, I have acquired a large number of carving tools. From these I select whichever I need for a particular job, one at a time, as the work requires. Although I have my old favourites, unless the work is a straight repeat, the tools that appear on the bench are always changing with the work. The forms of carvings – their shapes, depths and profiles – are far more variable than those produced by turning. Carvings are not bound by axial rotation and volume, and over literally thousands of years carving tools have evolved to deal with all the possible problems encountered by carvers in the course of their work.

Thus, a huge range of woodcarving tools is available compared with what is on offer to woodturners. As a turner beginning to carve you will need to know your way around the parts of these carving tools and what you can do with them, even though you may only use a few (see Fig 3.1). Fortunately this is easier than it first appears, and the information which follows will help you pick what you need for the project you have in mind.

It is very important that you do not just go off and buy a lot of carving tools in the hope of using them. Newcomers to carving often start by asking the following questions: is it necessary to have a large number of carving tools? How many do I need, because they're not cheap and you do seem to need a lot? What are the best makes to buy?

It's true, there are a lot of woodcarving tools. The large numbers of chisels and gouges can be daunting at first. They are numerous because the shapes they are used to cut are numerous – shapes that are much more complicated three-dimensionally than those found in turning. Not only do beginners have to choose tools whose uses are not fully clear, they usually have to spend time sharpening them before they can be used, perhaps only to find that they were not quite what was wanted for the job in question.

There is no such thing as a 'kit' of carving tools; all carvers have different collections depending on their work. It is best not to buy a boxed set of tools, unless you are sure they are what you need. You can start with some of the carving tools recommended in this chapter or in the projects, and you can also begin with a *few* carving tools that you particularly like the look of, or could imagine yourself using. Then buy more as you need them, basing your choice on the ones you are already familiar with.

FIG. 3.1 PARTS OF A TYPICAL STRAIGHT, PARALLEL-SIDED GOUGE.

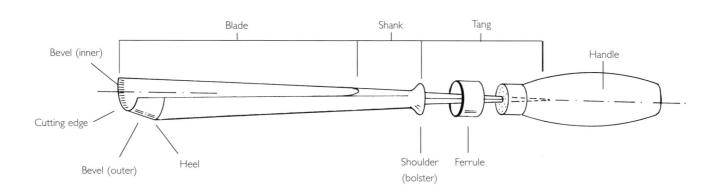

The important thing here is to *start*. And start with only a few tools. Then, using manufacturers' information (they all produce charts and pictures) choose the next tools you need based on the ones you already have. So: same shape as what you have, only wider, or narrower; same width only flatter or deeper; same width and shape only bent or fishtail, and so on.

You will end up with only those tools which suit exactly what *you* are doing, different from those of another carver. There is no lower or upper limit to the number you need – you need what you need to do the job.

In this book some tools will be found to be quite commonly used – the V tool for instance. Some may be used only once in a while. So it is not necessary to have a large kit of tools, only those *you* need to carve what *you* want to, as and when you know what you want to carve. Always buy your carving tools as you need them. A little experience will soon tell you what is necessary for a particular piece of work and, moving through the series of projects, you will see the different tools being used in various ways.

As to cost, it can add up alarmingly, certainly if you buy everything at once. But, as with turning, I bought my bits and pieces as I needed them and was surprised after a few years when I added it all up for insurance purposes. I look at buying both carving and turning tools in relative terms – relative to what else you can buy for the money. They may appear to cost a lot but represent very good value! I have carving tools over 100 years old with several names on the handles, still going strong. The years of pleasure, challenge and profit that they have brought to the hands that used them (including mine) is incalculable. Good carving tools, like all good tools, are nothing short of a good investment.

There are many good makes of carving tools on the market and you should always buy the best. Some makes which I can recommend are: Auriou, Pfeil, Henry Taylor, Bristol Design and Ashley Iles, all of whom regularly advertise in *Woodcarving* and other similar magazines. I always suggest that students select and try out the tools of a variety of manufacturers before settling for brand loyalty. All makes have strengths and weaknesses in both their forging and hardening, and all carvers have their own preferences.

Besides the greater variety of carving tools compared with turning tools, a second marked difference lies in the sharpening. It cannot be over-emphasized that *carving tools need really keen edges to produce the best work.* Normally, carving can be left straight from the chisels or gouges. Whether you prefer your carvings left in this manner or sanded is largely a matter of individual preference. But the actual process of carving itself is a much happier experience, and the product a much better piece of work, when the tools are razor sharp. Even when you wish to sand the finished surface, getting as close as you can to a satisfactory finish with the tools speeds up this part of the work; in my opinion, sanding is never enjoyable.

Blunt tools are frustrating to use, producing rough and scratched surfaces; they also need greater force to push them through the wood. Carvers spend more time and trouble on their carving tools than woodturners need to on theirs. As yet, woodcarving tools are not made of HSS; only high carbon steel can be forged into the complicated tool shapes. So you cannot treat carving tools like turning tools. Blueing the steel on a grinding wheel will ruin the temper and ability to hold a cutting edge.

Turners can find the time spent sharpening woodcarving tools a chore, putting them off carving – especially to begin with when they just want to get into the wood. But *do* stay with it. Follow the advice given later in this chapter and learn how to sharpen and maintain your cutting edges properly. You will find it will pay dividends in the long run; with practice it won't take too long to get lovely sharp edges, and the process will become almost second nature.

No matter how many tools you buy, or what level of carving you are interested in, do buy the best tools you can from a reliable manufacturer. Poor quality tools are a waste of time and money; good quality tools, sharpened and cared for, will last a lifetime.

Store your tools in a tool roll or drawer so that the edges are protected. Be careful when you are using the tools not to clash their edges together, or into metal clamps or parts of the lathe.

To summarize:

- Get to know your way around the different types of wood-carving tools and what they do.
- Start with a few, good quality, carving tools.
- Choose subsequent tools by working out what you need from what you have already.
- Learn to sharpen and maintain the cutting edges properly.
- Look after the delicate edges while you are using them, and store them carefully when you are not.

First to find our way around. There are three main 'families' of carving tools. If you look at any blade end-on, the cross-section of the cutting edge will be either flat, curved or angled.

Carving tool manufacturers in Britain use a traditional numbering system, called the Sheffield List, for referring to these edge cross-sections (see Fig 3.2). The system includes all the possible profiles in which carving tools are made, often laid out in a chart for reference. Some of the basic numbers will be noted as we go along. You will find that continental manufacturers use similar systems but normally stack the profiles into groups rather than lay them out as is usual in the UK. I personally find the continental way of depicting the shapes less useful, but the principle is the same. The best approach is to study the lists and details which all reputable manufacturers supply and be aware of differences. With a full-size chart you can place the edge of the tool on to its drawing and number it. From this you can work out whether you need a flatter or 'quicker' (more hollow) carving tool.

Let us now look at these cross-sections in more detail.

Flat

Flat carving tools are called **firmer chisels**. They differ from normal woodworking chisels in having bevels on both sides which place the cutting edge in the centre of the metal. If the edge is skewed, somewhere around 45°, you have a familiar-looking **skew chisel**. The firmer chisel is numbered 1 (01) and the skew 2 (02) in the Sheffield system.

Curved

Curved edges are based on varying arcs from smaller or larger circles. This sort of curve is properly known as the *sweep*. The cutting edge will indeed cut a true circle if presented to the wood vertically and allowed to follow its own track. These tools are the **gouges.** Gouges vary from very *flat* (a number 3) to greater amounts of curvature, said to be *quicker*. Eventually the cutting edge is shaped as a true semicircle (a number 9). Between these are a series of five other sweeps, moving between the flat and the semicircular (see Fig 3.3).

Some gouges have a U-shaped section with side walls rising from the semicircular base. These tools are more properly called **veiners** or **fluters** (numbers 10 and 11), veiners being quite small. An

NUMBER

Straight Tools	Long Bent Tools	Short Bent Tools	Back Bent Tools	2 1/16	3 1/8	5 3/16	6 1/4	8 5/16	10 3/8	11 7/16	13 1/2	14 9/16	16 5/8	20 3/4	22 7/8
1	–	21	–												
2	–	22	–												
3	12	24	33												
4	13	25	34												
5	14	26	35												
6	15	27	36												
7	16	28	37												
8	17	29	38												
9	18	30	–												
10	19	31	–												
11	20	32	–												
39	40	43	–												
41	42	44	–												
45	46	–	–												

CARVING TOOL SHAPES & PROFILES

26	30	32	36	38	MM
1	1⅛	1¼	1⅜	1½	Ins

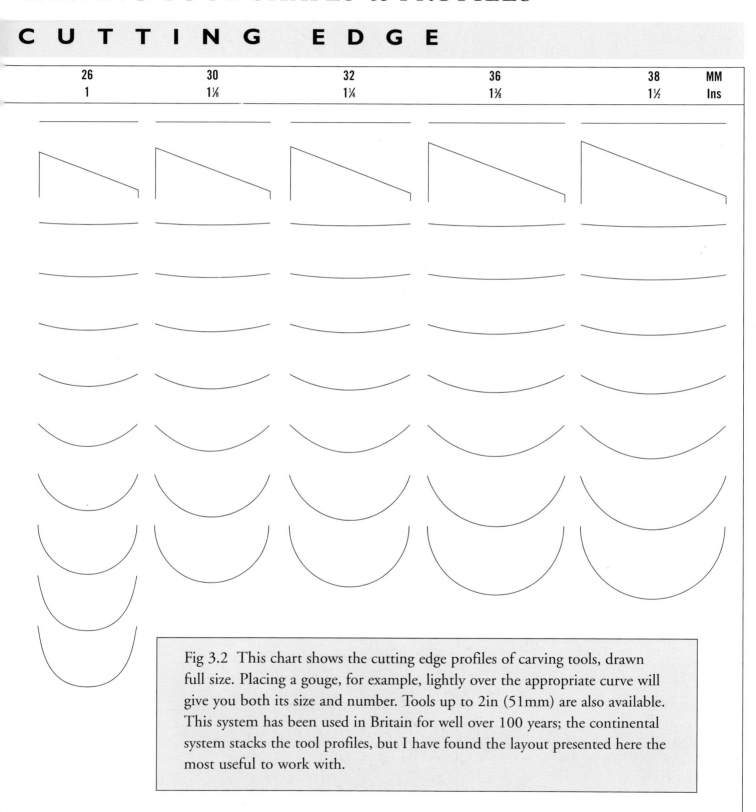

Fig 3.2 This chart shows the cutting edge profiles of carving tools, drawn full size. Placing a gouge, for example, lightly over the appropriate curve will give you both its size and number. Tools up to 2in (51mm) are also available. This system has been used in Britain for well over 100 years; the continental system stacks the tool profiles, but I have found the layout presented here the most useful to work with.

important difference is that these U-shaped tools will not follow an arc-like track as described above, nor can they be rocked through their cut.

Angled

The commonest of these tools, and by far the most useful, is the **V tool** (sometimes known as a **parting tool**). This resembles two chisels joined at an angle. This angle can be either 45°, 60° or 90° and, of these, the 60° is the one to start with.

Having differentiated these three families of shapes in your mind, consider two changes which a manufacturer can make to a carving tool:

- Change the shape along the *length* of the blade.
- Change the *width* across the cutting edge.

It is these permutations to the overall shape of the blade which produce the vast, and sometimes confusing, array of carving tools.

Longitudinal shape

- **The blade may be straight along its length, with parallel sides**
  These are the most common and useful shape of all carving tools.

Fig 3.3 The inside curvature, or 'sweep', of gouges ranges from very flat to semicircular; they can also be U-shaped.

- **The blade may be straight, but with varying amounts of splay or spread towards the cutting edge**

    When the blade starts spreading from the shoulder, the tool is known as an **allongee**. Tools that have a long shank with a sudden taper towards the cutting end are known as **fishtails** (see Fig 3.4). Those blades in between, with some shank before splaying, are known as **spade** tools. Gouges and chisels are available in both allongee and fishtail forms,   but not V tools.

- **The blade may curve shallowly, towards the front, along the whole length of the blade**

    These are known variously as **longbent, curved** or **swan-neck** tools (see Fig 3.5). Different manufacturers make tools with different amounts of bend – you will be able to assess whether the amount of curve in a particular make will do the job you want it to do.

- **The blade may curve tightly in the part of blade towards the cutting end, leaving a length of square shank**

    These are known as **shortbent**, **front bent**, **spoon** or **spoonbit** tools (see Fig 3.6). As with the longbent tools, the amount of bend varies between makers. Chisels, V tools and gouges are all available in a **shortbent** form. Shortbent skew chisels are often

FIG 3.4 SOME LONGITUDINAL SHAPES OF CARVING TOOLS. THE TWO ON THE LEFT ARE LONGBENT, THE NEXT THREE SHORTBENT AND THE TWO ON THE RIGHT ARE FISHTAILS.

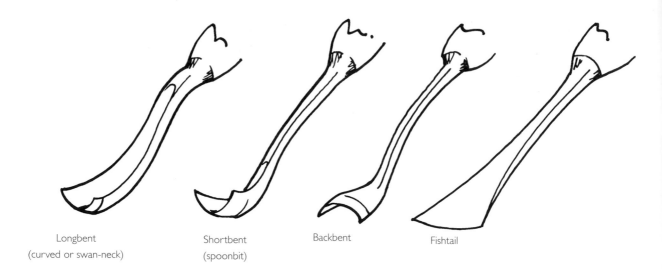

Longbent
(curved or swan-neck)

Shortbent
(spoonbit)

Backbent

Fishtail

FIG 3.5 SOME SHAPES ALONG THE
LENGTH OF WOODCARVING TOOLS.

called **corner chisels** – the edge can point to the left or the
right, and they are usually bought in pairs.

- **The blade may bend tightly, but in the opposite direction
  to the shortbent tools**
  These are **backbent** tools – usually gouges. V tools are not
  made in this form.

The reasons for all the different shapes will be explained in the next
section which looks at their functions.

WIDTH

Any of these tools can be bought in a range of widths, which are
measured from corner to corner of a chisel, across the blade of a

FIG 3.6 THE SHORTBENT GOUGE.
THIS TOOL WILL CUT DEEPER
HOLLOWS THAN ITS STRAIGHT
EQUIVALENT.

skew, and corner to corner across the mouth of a gouge (see Fig 3.7).

Sizes can vary from delicate tools of ⅟₃₂in (1mm) up to a massive 2in (51mm) for sculpture gouges or lettering chisels. The size of any tool that you need is again dictated by the work you want to produce, but do remember that you can often make the work of one tool do that of another.

Chisels

Chisels will most obviously cut straight lines – as in lettering – but they will also smooth slightly rounded surfaces.

Skew chisels

The long point of the skew is used to clean into otherwise inaccessible corners. Bear in mind that the longer the point, the more fragile – do not rock the blade sideways in its cut or you will snap the point off. The skew will also chase curves and smooth rounded surfaces – particularly useful in low relief.

Shortbent corner chisels are able to get into recessed corners, to the left or right, and clean them up.

V tools

A lot of decorative lines and marks can be made with the V tool, even hair and feathers. These tools will outline those areas which are to be relieved from their background in relief carving, cleaning up angles and junctions. The three different angles of V tool available simply give different sorts of cut. The narrowest angle is very useful

FIG 3.7 THE WIDTHS OF A PARTICULAR SWEEP OF GOUGE CAN VARY FROM VERY SMALL TO VERY LARGE.

for undercutting.

In this book there are only two projects which do not use the V tool – so it is certainly worth mastering its use and rather tricky sharpening.

Gouges

Gouges are used from start to finish in carving: from initial roughing out to the final finished surface, they remove wood, model surfaces, shape edges and make decorative or meaningful marks. The sweep of a gouge can also be used to match specific curves in repeat patterns and mouldings. Fluters and veiners run deeper channels and can be used in relief carving instead of V tools.

Fishtail tools

Having more prominent corners than the normal parallel-sided gouges or chisels, fishtails can get into corners more easily. Like the skew the corners of fishtails are delicate, and the tapered shape makes them become narrower as they are sharpened. Use them for lighter, more delicate work and finishing. Allongee and spade tools are lighter to work with and improve surface visibility; they are somewhat larger and tougher than the fishtail shape and can be seen as a compromise between the parallel-sided and fishtail tools.

Long and shortbent tools

The varying degrees of curve along the length of carving tools enable recesses and hollows to be worked where a straight tool would foul the wood. In practice I find myself opting for the short bend rather than the long one, but this is personal preference. Longer bends deal with shallower curves and hollows and the shorter bends are suitable for tighter ones.

Flat gouges or chisels are called **grounders** or **grounding tools**, and are extremely useful for cleaning the background in relief carving.

Backbent gouges

Backbent gouges are used to enter hollows with the edge in an 'upside down' position.

I am often asked to recommend a 'starting set' of woodcarving tools. Most manufacturers do put tools together under such a title but, as I have said, because the individual's choice of work, and hence their needs, are endless I don't think buying a boxed set of tools is the best approach. No doubt if you have bought or been given such a boxed set of tools they will be useful sooner or later, but it is best to choose your tools on the basis of need, not on what the manufacturers wish to market.

However, back me into a corner and I may say, among other things, that the tools shown in Table 3.1 are very often on my bench. Choosing from among these is probably as good a place as any to start if you have no idea what you want, and all of them appear at some point in the projects.

CHOOSING YOUR FIRST CARVING TOOLS

No.	Width		Description
	ins	mm	
01	¼	6	Straight (firmer) chisel
01	½	13	Straight (firmer) chisel
02	⅜	10	Skew (corner) chisel
03	¼	6	Flat gouge (straight)
04	½	13	Flat gouge (straight)
06	¼	6	Medium gouge (straight)
06	½	13	Medium gouge (straight)
06	¾	19	Medium gouge (straight)
09	¼	6	Quick gouge (straight)
09	½	13	Quick gouge (straight)
11	3⁄16	5	Fluter (straight)
39	¼	6	Parting (V) tool

TABLE 3.1 USEFUL CARVING TOOLS FOR THE BEGINNER.

Consider also bent and fishtail tools in any of these sweeps and sizes.

The number refers to the Sheffield List. With firms not using this system, you will have to make comparisons from the catalogue information of the maker.

HANDLING AND USING CARVING TOOLS

As you look through this book, pay attention to the various hand positions shown, the way the tools are being held and the grips being used. There are two very common ways of holding and manipulating carving tools:

- The basic two-handed grip (see Fig 3.8) involves wrapping one hand around the shoulder of the blade – this hand has a braking, controlling function – and the other gripping the end of the handle – propelling, rotating and manipulating. This position is a strong one suitable for most work, including long and strong cuts.
- What I call the 'pen and dagger' grip (see Fig 3.9) involves holding the blade like a pen in one hand – working mainly with the fingers to control and manipulate – and gripping the handle like a dagger with the other, propelling and manipulating.

With both these grips note that one hand is *always* resting on the work and that movement and control of the tool lies in a combination of *both hands* working together. Chapter 4 deals with decorating the surface of a piece of work and gives simple and basic exercises in holding and cutting with carving tools. Also, do be sure to follow the safety advice which appears later in this chapter; this

FIG 3.8 THE TWO-HANDED GRIP: THE BLADE HAND AROUND THE SHANK, THUMB ON THE HANDLE, RESTING ON THE WORKPIECE; THE OTHER HAND PROPELLING FROM THE BACK. BOTH HANDS ARE USED TO CONTROL THE TOOL AS IT CUTS THE WOOD.

FIG 3.9 THE 'PEN AND DAGGER' GRIP: ONE HAND HOLDING THE BLADE LIKE A PEN AND RESTING ON THE WORK; THE OTHER GRIPPING THE HANDLE LIKE A DAGGER. BOTH HANDS CONTROL AND MANIPULATE THE TOOL.

FIG 3.8

FIG 3.9

includes safe ways of working and precautions against accidents.

Tools may be bought roughly 'set' by grinding, but not sharpened, or more frequently these days, 'pre-sharpened', where the manufacturer has put an edge on them for you. However, as these pre-sharpened tools still get blunt, they will have to be sharpened at some time or other, so there is no getting away from the necessity of learning how to sharpen woodcarving chisels and gouges correctly.

Let me repeat, you must aim at producing seriously keen edges to your carving tools to get the best results. Even if you find sharpening difficult to start with, try your best, and try to improve the edge every time you sharpen it. With a little practice you will soon have the edge in a fine condition.

It has been my experience of turners who take up carving that they are thrown by the subtleties of sharpening carving tools. They are so used to whipping their turning tools across a grinding wheel and going straight back to the wood on the lathe that they have a crude approach to sharpening. By this I am not being derogatory – it is exactly what *I* do, and is an appropriate sharpening method when cutting wood on the lathe. But it is entirely inappropriate to carving tools and the chances are that, as a turner, you will have to consciously be more patient in this area and take things slowly.

SHARPENING CARVING TOOLS

Fig 3.10 Basic equipment for sharpening carving tools: coarse Carborundum (part of a combination stone) at the back, Arkansas benchstone, slip stones and light oil.

One of my students, who started rather heavy handed, found that chanting 'just a touch, just a touch' as he approached the final sharp cutting edge helped him remain aware of what he was doing and prevented him oversharpening, ending up with a crumpled edge, and needing to start again.

Equipment

You will need:

- A coarse Carborundum benchstone (or a combination fine and coarse stone) for preliminary sharpening.
- A fine, white (translucent) Arkansas stone for the final edge.
- A few slip stones of both Carborundum and Arkansas. Slip stones are used to remove the burr on the inside of gouges and V tools, or to form a proper inner bevel, and can be bought in sets (see Figs 3.10 and 3.11).
- A strop of hard leather impregnated with a fine abrasive or proprietary stropping paste. A strop around 4in (102mm) wide by 10in (254mm) long is a good size.
- Some slipstrops made of thin leather glued to shaped pieces of wood and dressed with abrasive. The inside face of a carving tool is stropped to match the stropping on the outside.
- Light oil for the stones. Always use plenty of oil to float away the grit particles from the surface of the stone and prevent it clogging.

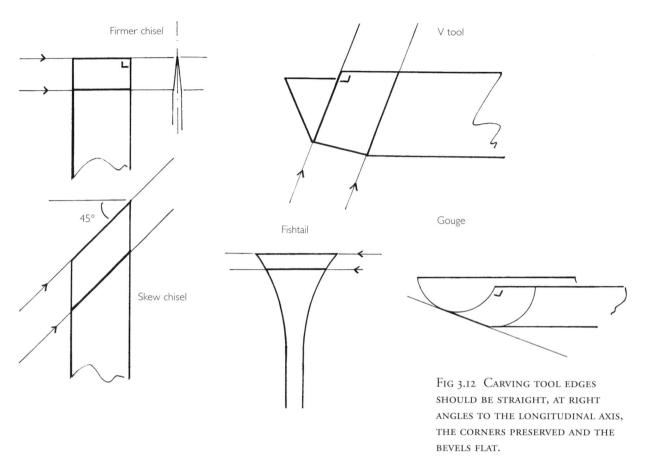

Firmer chisel

V tool

45°

Fishtail

Skew chisel

Gouge

FIG 3.12 CARVING TOOL EDGES
SHOULD BE STRAIGHT, AT RIGHT
ANGLES TO THE LONGITUDINAL AXIS,
THE CORNERS PRESERVED AND THE
BEVELS FLAT.

You probably already have a bench grinder that you use on turning tools. Remember that carving tool steel must never get more than warm – so dip the blades in cold water frequently if you need to grind them, and go carefully, applying only a light pressure.

General guide to sharpening

A correctly sharpened carving tool has the following features (see Fig 3.12).

- A *flat bevel*, not hollow, not rounded and with no secondary bevels. Grind an angle of about 20–30° – more for harder woods and less for softwoods.
- A *straight edge* from corner to corner, at *right angles* to the axis of the blade (except the skew chisel). Set this straight edge first by offering the blade perpendicularly to the bench stone.
- *Corners* preserved for use – especially on skew and fishtail tools.

The cutting edge of a dull tool, if you look end-on, will show a white line of light, which will get thinner and vanish completely as the tool becomes sharp. Use this white line as your guide at all times; it tells you from where metal needs to be removed and – equally important – where metal needs to be left untouched by the bench stones.

The secret is to keep an eye constantly on the state of this white line, pushing the edge into a piece of softwood occasionally to remove any wire burr, and proceeding evenly. A tool may need some preliminary shaping on the grinder, and can then be refined on the coarse Carborundum stone. From here move to the Arkansas stone. Keep the white line even, the bevel flat on the stone, and be careful not to wear away the corners.

A sharp tool produces a polished cut with no scratch marks. If there are any rough points or trails when you test your edge on a piece of waste wood, look at the edge for a tell-tale spot of light and carefully touch up this part before testing again.

We can now look more specifically at sharpening the different types of tool.

Chisels

Sharpen with the end of the stone towards you. Keep the bevels equal so the cutting edge lies in the centre. Keep the bevel flat by not

FIG 3.13 SHARPENING THE FIRMER CHISEL EQUALLY ON BOTH SIDES.

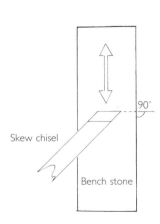

FIG 3.14 SHARPENING A SKEW CHISEL ON A BENCH STONE, REVERSING FOR THE BEVEL ON THE OTHER SIDE.

raising or lowering the handle (see Fig 3.13). Work on the Carborundum stone until the white line is a little more than a hair's thickness, then finish on the Arkansas stone. Strop the tool on both sides equally, *dragging* the edge on the leather so as not to cut the strop. Skew chisels should be presented at an angle to the stone (see Fig 3.14).

V tools

These are probably the trickiest carving tools to sharpen but are among the most useful, so I will look at the sharpening of these tools in a bit more detail.

V tools are best treated as two chisels joined at one edge to form a cutting angle (see Fig 3.15). As such they *should* present no more trouble than the chisels themselves. However, the angle needs special treatment as it is a thicker piece of metal and it is getting this V angle right that causes the most problems. These arise mainly from improper, or too hasty, shaping at the grinding stage, inaccurate application of the bevel to the bench stone, or too vigorous use of the slip stones in the angle.

The V apex between the sides is not strictly a sharp angle but

FIG 3.15 SHARPENING THE V TOOL. IT IS IMPORTANT TO SHARPEN EACH SIDE OF THE TOOL EQUALLY.

slightly rounded. This is not particularly noticeable unless you examine the groove cut by the V tool closely, but this slight rounding allows the tool to negotiate corners more easily. The keel itself remains straight. It is crucial that the cutting apex and edges of the V tool (the parts which leave the finished cut) are properly sharp, otherwise a ragged cut is inevitable.

As mentioned before, the secret of successful sharpening is to allow the white line to be a guide to metal thickness and use the bevel scratches to tell you how the metal is being presented to the stone.

Specially shaped, angle-edged slip stones are used to clean off the wire edge inside the angle. The slip stone must fit *exactly* into the corner. It is easy to work the slip more to one side of the angle than in the centre, creating a notch.

This is the method I use to sharpen the V tool:

Grind the edges square, with the V tool perpendicular to the grinding wheel. If the tool was supplied nosed, the edges will now look like two wedges, thickening to the angle. Follow this with one or two perpendicular passes on the Arkansas stone to clean and refine the white line.

Set the keel angle by presenting the tool across the wheel – an average angle would be about 20°. The keel angle is the central junction of the two sides, along the bevel. You may find with larger V tools that the thicker metal at the junction of the two sides means the keel ends up longer than the side bevels. Reduce the thickness of the white line at the apex to about 1/16in (2mm). The outside corner of the angle will look cut off.

The next step is to set the bevel angles on the wheel, treating each side of the tool in turn like a chisel and rendering the white lines to the same 1/16in (2mm) thickness. The heel should be parallel with the cutting edges, and the V apex aligned dead in the centre. End-on, the angle will still look slightly cut off.

Position the bench stones end-on and use angled slip stones for the inside. Start reducing the thickness of the edge down to 1/32in (1mm) with the Carborundum, then switch to the Arkansas stone, working each side equally. There is always a tendency to over-sharpen the corners, being thinner than the central parts. If the white line that illuminates the edge thins at any point, slightly turn the wrist to exert a little more pressure on the thicker part of the edge and away from the thinner part. Take great care to keep the bevels flat, use the white line and bevel scratches to help you decide exactly how the tool should be presented to the stone, and remember to push the edge into scrap wood occasionally to remove any wire burr.

As the white line thins and disappears on the Arkansas stone, a point of light will be left at the apex; usually the apex projects a little to form a hook. This is due to the thicker metal at the junction. To remove this, turn the Arkansas stone side-on and lay the keel flat on the surface. Rock the tool from side to side and very carefully hone the keel until the spot of light, or hook, disappears. Do not overwork the keel as this will dip the apex back. Any remaining spots of light can be removed with the slip stone.

Finally, cut across some softwood grain to test the edge, strop inside and out (using a shaped internal slipstrop) and carefully wipe the blade.

Gouges

Sharpen these tools with the bench stone side-on. Present the bevel flat with the handle in one hand and two fingers of the other hand a little above the cutting edge. Start at one end with the gouge turned so that its mouth points towards the centre of the stone (see Fig 3.16). As you move the gouge to the other end of the stone rotate the handle from the wrist to arrive on the opposite corner of the gouge, again with the mouth pointing into the stone. Reverse this action to achieve a smooth rotation from side to side, without raising or lowering the handle, using gentle but firm pressure (see Fig 3.17). How much rotation is needed depends on the curvature of the gouge. Use a slip stone that matches the internal shape of the gouge to work some inside bevel, throwing the cutting edge towards the centre of the metal. This makes the edge tougher, relieves the chips more easily and helps when the tool is used upside down (see Fig

FIG 3.16 START THE GOUGE AT END SIDE OF THE STONE WITH THE BEVEL LYING FLAT.

FIG 3.17 FINISH AT THE OTHER END OF THE STONE AFTER ROTATING THE BLADE. REPEAT THE ACTION IN THE OPPOSITE DIRECTION WITHOUT LIFTING THE BLADE FROM THE STONE.

FIG 3.18 SLIP STONING A GOUGE – CHOOSE A SLIP THAT MATCHES THE SWEEP OF THE GOUGE.

FIG 3.16

FIG 3.17

FIG 3.18

FIG 3.19 STROP THE GOUGE WITH A
ROTATING ACTION TO COVER ALL THE
EDGE – LIFT THE GOUGE ON THE
RETURN STROKE.

FIG 3.20 A SLIPSTROP OF BENT
LEATHER USED FOR THE INSIDE OF
THE GOUGE – PUSH AWAY FROM THE
EDGE TO AVOID A DIG IN.

FIG 3.19

FIG 3.20

FIG 3.21 THE SHARPNESS OF THIS V
TOOL IS OBVIOUS AS IT IS USED TO
CUT GROOVES.

3.18). Strop with a rotating action when the white line of light has disappeared, using a slipstrop on the inside (see Figs 3.19 and 3.20).

All other tools are variations on these basic shapes (flat and curved). You will need to experiment a little with the curved and bent profiles to find a comfortable way of holding them, so as to present the bevel correctly and accurately to the bench stone.

As you carve, you must keep your tools slick by stropping them regularly. If scratch marks or dullness appears, look for tell-tale white spots on the edge and touch up straight away (see Fig 3.21).

There are various electrical machines on the market which use belts and buffing wheels to sharpen carving tools. It is not that easy to work to the criteria of straight bevels and keeping the corners with such machines, while at the same time it *is* easy to oversharpen and remove corners. Such equipment is also quite expensive when compared with the few bench stones you need, bearing in mind that you may only wish to undertake a small amount of carving in any case. My advice for newcomers is always to learn to sharpen carving tools carefully with bench and slip stones, then to *try* such sharpening machines once they really know what they are doing, and certainly before buying such equipment.

ACCESSORY TOOLS

Besides the array of tools specifically for woodcarving, carvers use many other tools common to all woodworkers. Saws, especially those for cutting curves, rasps, spokeshaves and drills are all the type of tool most woodturners already have and, depending on the type of carving work they have in mind, will generally be useful here too (see Fig 3.22).

There are two other tools more particular to carving that are worth pointing out: **rifflers** and **punches**.

FIG 3.22 SURFORM RASPS, FILES AND RIFFLERS (TO THE RIGHT) USED BY CARVERS TO SHAPE WOOD.

Rifflers

These are double-ended, paddle-shaped rasps that are used to clean up awkward areas. If a carver is doing a lot of shaped work they might be used quite extensively along with other rasps and files, before finishing with sandpaper. They come in a range of shapes and sizes.

Punches

These are short pieces of cylindrical or hexagonal steel with a shaped end, used to indent and pattern the surface of the wood, and some will appear in the projects. **Frosters** or **frosting tools** are punches with many-toothed, hatched ends used to texture or decorate a surface, and you can make many of them yourself. Use them sparingly, and *never* to disguise an otherwise rough surface.

Mallets

Mallets used by woodcarvers are cylindrical and made from dense woods such as lignum vitae. If you are only undertaking light carving you may never actually need one (see Fig 3.23). Making a mallet is a fairly straightforward piece of turning and I described the process in issue 12 of *Woodturning* magazine.

FIG 3.23 MALLETS, PATTERNED
PUNCHES AND A FLEXIBLE SHAFT —
ACCESSORY TOOLS FOR THE CARVER.

Electrical tools

Of all the electrical tools, the bandsaw is probably the most useful to the carver as well as the turner. Another piece of equipment increasingly finding favour is the high speed flexible shaft. This holds a range of cutters and burrs for shaping the wood rather than carving it, and will appear in Chapter 4 when it is used to make some decorative marks. As they are quite expensive, it would be best to try one first. Always protect yourself from dust and the danger of flying particles, and treat the cutters and burrs gently.

HOLDING WORK OFF THE LATHE

Carvers use all sorts of holding devices to help them get at the work safely, happily improvising where necessary. Examples of vices, clamps and holdfasts being used will appear throughout the projects. Some work, as mentioned in the previous chapter, can be carved on the lathe, but other work is best handled on a workbench.

Good access to the workpiece is essential and I have found swivel ball adjustable clamps excellent for many purposes but, as with all things, their cost has to be weighed against their usefulness.

You will see cheaper means of holding work in this book, one of the cheapest being a **carver's screw** which inserts into the workpiece and passes through a hole in the bench to be tightened up from

underneath with a fly (see Fig 3.24). **Carver's chops** are vices which mount above the bench and can swivel to adjust the working position.

Try and work out how you intend to hold your work right at the start; you may, for example, be able to make use of a spigot or other waste wood that can be removed later.

Carving tools should be razor sharp and as such they need to be manipulated safely. It is lack of concentration and forethought that cause most mishaps while working. Safety lies in maintaining *control* of the carving tools and carving process.

Here are some simple rules that will enable you to carve safely – *do* follow them.

SAFETY

- **The workpiece must always be held securely to a stable bench or worksurface**

  If the workpiece moves unpredictably, control is lost and an accident may happen. Only the cutting edge should move, while the workpiece remains fixed – the opposite of woodturning. Check that everything is firm before starting to carve, and periodically as you work.

- **Keep both hands, and fingers, *behind* the cutting edge at all times**
As it is only the actual cutting edge which is sharp, it follows that it is impossible to be cut if you keep your hands and fingers in this position.

- **All carving tools should be held with both hands**
Two excellent ways to work with carving tools were mentioned above. Both involved one hand on the handle, the other wrapped around the blade or shank, behind the cutting edge – safe, controlled positions. The *only* exception to this 'two hands on' rule is when you use a mallet.

- **The heel of the blade hand should rest on the workpiece at all times**
This position increases control of the carving tool as it cuts, adding to safety.

- **Never cut or exert pressure towards *any* part of the body**
Carving tools are offered to the wood at many different angles; occasionally you must reposition the work to avoid carving dangerously.

- **Maintain your carving tools in the sharpest possible condition**
As you must push the carving tool to cut the wood fibres, a blunt cutting edge needs far more pressure to move it through the material. The tool tends to jerk out of the wood at the end of its cut and into the air – uncontrollably. A sharp tool is safer because it cuts cleanly and with less effort. This is contrary to what most people think about bluntness.

- **Never lay carving tools down with their cutting edges projecting**
You may have many chisels and gouges in use at any one time, and all should be laid down and picked up safely. Unused tools are best laid out of harm's way, flat, in a row towards the back of the work area. Edges normally point towards the carver to help recognition. This organized treatment of tools also protects the delicate cutting edges from clashing together.

- **Always wear footwear strong enough to protect your feet**
  In the affray of carving it is possible to drop your chisel, gouge, or another object, or knock one off the bench. Foot protection is therefore essential.

- **Never try to catch a falling woodcarving tool**
  It doesn't take long to resharpen an edge if it gets damaged, far quicker than the healing of a cut hand or finger. Attempting to catch a tool is a difficult event to guard against as there is a natural reflex to try and stop, or catch, something falling. But you must step back quickly and let it go.

- **Keep the hand supporting the strop to one side and well out of the way of the return, forward stroke**
  As stropping is a regular activity, this hazard reappears continually. Remember that the sharp edge passes through the air towards the starting position on the leather. Don't rush stropping but take it easy and carefully.

Let us move move on to discuss what makes a good carving. Of course, the following are my own opinions and hence contentious but, starting with technique: carved work should be cleanly cut without torn or rough grain. This means that the carving tools must be properly – in other words extremely – sharp. The cuts themselves should be confident and meaningful with the shapes of the cutting edges doing the work.

The design should combine the carving with the turning in a 'natural', unforced manner and be appropriate to the wood in which it is embodied. Lines and profiles should flow.

A final surface that is filed or sanded *still needs to have been carved well in the first place*. Remember, injudicious sanding can cause a piece of carving to resemble a partly sucked boiled sweet. Sharp carving tools, carefully and precisely used, will give a unique final appearance to your work. Never rasp or sand as an attempt to disguise poor use of the tools; far better to try again.

WHAT MAKES GOOD CARVING?

CHAPTER 4

Decorative marks I

SUN BOWL

This chapter will look at one of the commonest ways in which turners use carving tools – to decorate the surface, or edge, of a bowl or plate. Here the cuts that are left from tools are used to pattern the surface of the wood in various deliberate ways. But since carvers also use punches, files and, more and more, high speed rotary burrs and cutters in their work, these too need to be mentioned as being available for the use of the turner in achieving a decorative effect. The chapter will end with a simple decorated bowl project which uses tool marks in this way.

I use the term 'decorative marks' to contrast with other carving approaches, in that it is the cuts of the tools themselves which are important – the tools are not used in the normal way to remove wood and reveal, or represent, a subject. The term could cover the laying down of a few simple cuts, or repeat patterns, or surface texturing, where simple marks are built up into abstract areas. In the next chapter the cuts become more representational.

I would like to begin with a few thoughts about using decorative cuts and surface texturing before moving on to practising them.

A while ago, before the surge in popularity, it was relatively rare to see turned work that was not a frank exercise in woodturning, or straightforwardly, even clearly, made of wood. One reason for the change in fashion is the natural creativeness of human beings, which will always manifest itself if conditions allow, and continually push at boundaries and limits. Another reason is the desire to be different for the sake of being noticed, or a restless inability to appreciate or achieve simple beauty. Strangely, both positive and negative motivations can give rise to fine, engaging work, as well as pretentious and overworked pieces.

As I mentioned in Chapter 2, I feel it is very important for turners to achieve a good level of competence in straightforward turning – through working at it, even within a limited range. So, my first point is that it is poor practice to use texturing to disguise a poorly turned surface.

Second, I always encourage students to be content with the simple beauties of wood and form first, before introducing skills from other crafts. The best approach is to spread from basic roots, like a tree. The tree is still recognizable as a unity, and for us the analogy is one of a unity of intention, and a sense that wood is still our primary medium.

A final point is to recognize how a piece 'works'. In other words, what effect your decoration of the edge or surface of a turning has on the eye of the viewer. I mean here the effect of proportions and weight; the balance of plane to texture; the contrast between one part of the shape and another, and so on. The piece of work will be changing, and even though aesthetics is a subjective, personal world, there is a lot of consensus and shared perception. For example you must balance the amount of texturing to the lip of a bowl with the sense of space left elsewhere. My approach is to try to think myself into another's shoes and feel what is happening from an unbiased viewpoint – which is not that easy.

MAKING MARKS

Before attempting anything on a time-consuming piece of turning, I suggest that you get a strip of clean hardwood, clamp it to a bench and use it for practice. Make the strip 2–3in (51–76mm) wide and divide its length into units of similar dimensions. Experiment with different marks, cuts and textures within the units and keep the results as a record. You can of course use different woods, and add colours, try burning effects, or wire-wool, to see what other effects you can achieve. Make a note of what you did on the back of the practice piece as you are likely to have forgotten a hundred textures later! These strips will be a useful resource for future work.

The wood I used in this project was English oak, and you will see that some of the effects have problems – such as the open fibres of the grain tending to crumble. Finding this sort of thing out is the point of the exercise in the first place.

Remember that when a surface is cut or torn through texturing it will affect the appearance of any stains and polishes that are applied, as the light will now be reflected differently.

FIG 4.1 THE FOREDOM HIGH SPEED
FLEXIBLE DRIVE WITH MOTOR, SHAFT
AND HANDPIECE; FOOT PEDAL FOR
SPEED ADJUSTMENT; COLLETS,
LOCKING SPANNER AND THREE
ASSORTED CUTTING BURRS.

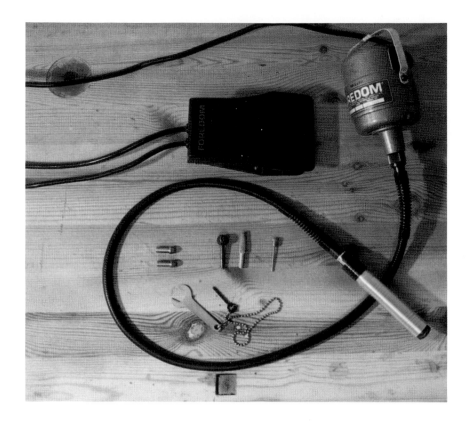

High speed flexible drives

These machines consist of a motor which is suspended near the work
area and which drives a handpiece through a flexible shaft (see Fig
4.1). The handpiece can be fitted with a wide range of burrs, cutters
and drills and is used to shape and texture the wood (see Fig 4.2).
The speed, which can be as high as a normal router, can be varied
with a foot pedal.

High speed flexible drives are gaining popularity among many
carvers, and some use nothing else when shaping their work (by my
definition in Chapter 1). Very delicate and excellent work is possible,
though there are limitations, and they are more frequently used in

FIG 4.2 CLOSE-UP OF A FEW OF THE
LARGE RANGE OF BURRS, DRILLS AND
CUTTERS THAT ARE AVAILABLE FOR
HIGH SPEED DRIVES.

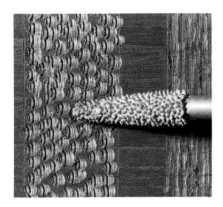

FIG 4.3

FIG 4.4

FIG 4.5

combination with carving tools to achieve the desired effect, after which the piece is usually finished with sandpaper. You may find these machines helpful in shaping your work but do remember that the effect they give is quite different from that produced by toolwork.

Such equipment is quite expensive, creates dust and *must* be used with eye protection and face mask; all this needs to be balanced against its usefulness. A make which can be recommended is Foredom, but do try and have a go on one first, as for many users the shape and feel of the handpiece is the important factor.

Figs 4.3, 4.4 and 4.5 show examples of texturing with a high speed flexible drive. I touched the tip of a rough, conical-shaped burr to the practice wood in Fig 4.3 creating a series of crescents which could be overlapped like fish scales. With a parallel, finer burr I drew a series of lines in the next practice section, shown in Fig 4.4. You can see how the burr essentially tears the surface of the wood as it rotates at high speed. In the next experiment, shown in Fig 4.5, I kept the same burr and held the handpiece vertically so that the tip rotated around a point and produced neat rings in the wood.

So, with little difficulty, three textures. Many more effects are possible, and many other burrs available for use, with discretion, on turnings.

Punches and frosters

Figs 4.6, 4.7 and 4.8 show a similar series of texturing using carver's punches and a froster. A punch is a shaped point used to indent a surface or clean up a particular carved hollow, and punches are used in some of the projects later in this book. Many different shapes are available, the simplest of which you can often make yourself.

FIGS 4.3, 4.4 & 4.5 DIFFERENT MARKS CAN BE MADE WITH DIFFERENT CUTTERS PRESENTED IN DIFFERENT WAYS. NOTE HOW THE WOOD IS EFFECTIVELY TORN.

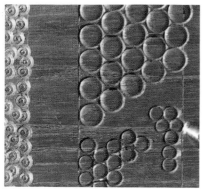

FIG 4.6

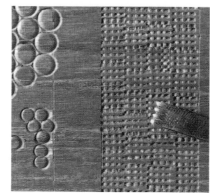

FIG 4.7

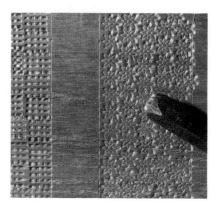

FIG 4.8

FIGS 4.6, 4.7 & 4.8 PUNCHES AND
FROSTERS CRUNCH WOOD FIBRES
INTO SHAPE. DIFFERENT WOODS
WILL ACCEPT THIS TREATMENT
IN DIFFERENT WAYS.

FIG 4.9 TEXTURING WITH A
V TOOL.

FIG 4.10 SIMPLE CUTS WITH
DIFFERENT CARVING TOOLS. AGAIN
THE QUALITIES OF THE WOOD AND
CLEAN CUTTING ARE IMPORTANT.

Fig 4.6 shows how different sizes of circular punches will pattern a surface; you can also see how the smaller punch crumbled the open grain of the wood. This is the sort of thing the test piece is meant to reveal. The circular punch is one of the most useful punches for the trade carver.

'Frosters' are essentially punches which have a cross-hatched working end. Again these will be seen elsewhere in the book. Fig 4.7 shows a regular pattern laid down on the test piece, which can of course be varied. The effect is something like a shadow when seen from a distance. These tools are easy to make by filing the end of a large nail.

Fig 4.8 shows a more decorative flower pattern punch being used. Covering a surface with this sort of punch is hardly more effective

FIG 4.9

FIG 4.10

FIG 4.11

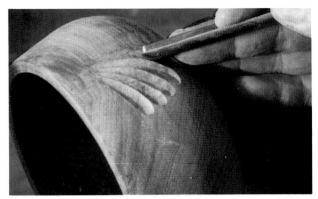

FIG 4.12

than using a froster, and they are best used with discretion, leaving plenty of space for the pattern to be seen.

The most important thing I can say about these tools is that the surface to which they are applied needs to be clean and smooth. It is a mistake to use them to cover over a rough area; it never works well.

Carving tool marks

Fig 4.9 shows a V tool being used to texture my test piece. The cuts are across the grain and even though the tool is properly sharp you can see that there is a crumbling of the wood fibres wherever the grain is more open – this will be the summer wood part of the annual rings. The pattern would fare better if cut *with* the grain. These marks could be made longer or shorter, straight, bent, curly and so on. Any one woodcarving tool is capable of producing a range of marks and textures.

Fig 4.10 shows two sorts of marks, short and long, using a U-shaped gouge (number 11). Again crumbling is apparent. The lesson must be to suit the texturing to the wood or vice versa. With carving tools quite deep decorative marks are possible.

Fig 4.11 shows a few deep marks cut in a fan shape to the side of what was otherwise quite a plain and unexciting bowl. They were carved, with the bowl locked on the lathe, with a deep gouge (number 10 or 11) (see Fig 4.12). A touch of sandpaper to the sharp edges of the cuts was needed to make for a more pleasant feel to the hands. Many pieces will be handled and the tactile qualities should be pleasing whatever the work.

Although not dealt with here, remember that files, rasps, rifflers and many other tools, including power tools are also available for texturing and marking surfaces.

FIG 4.11 SIMPLE TOOL CUTS TO THE SIDE OF A PLAIN BOWL.

FIG 4.12 THE BOWL WAS CARVED ON THE LATHE WITH THE MANDREL LOCKED.

Project: Sun bowl

Turning

This simple project is an example of the use of decorative, texturing marks. It is an attempt to create an object in which the proportions of plain and patterned surfaces, space and mass, all 'work' together.

The bowl is turned in the normal way: first using a faceplate for the outside, then an adjustable chuck to grip the bowl from beneath to enable hollowing. The proportions are given as measurements in Fig 4.13.

FIG 4.13 WORKING DIMENSIONS OF THE PROJECT BOWL.

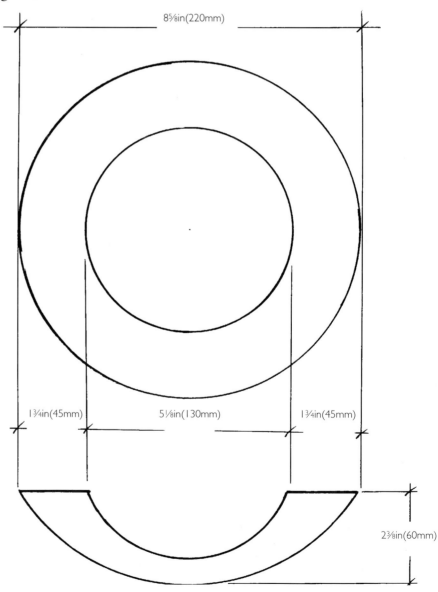

8⅝in(220mm)

1¾in(45mm)   5⅛in(130mm)   1¾in(45mm)

2⅜in(60mm)

The bowl has very thick walls, giving it a chunky appearance. The rim of the bowl is wide enough to show off the decorative marks. It is best to turn the rim as cleanly as possible first, carve it, then use a block with sandpaper to clean and smooth it. This way grit from the sandpaper does not take the edge off the tool.

Carving tools

Only one tool was necessary: a ¼in (6mm) medium V tool. A small U-shaped gouge would also have worked well, and it is worth mentioning a triangular file as an option in this context – so going from 'carving' to 'shaping'.

Carving

The bowl was held by the chuck which had been used to hold the work on the lathe. I used the same shaped-block gripping method which is seen in Chapter 14.

With a centre-finder I marked a few guiding, radial lines (see Fig 4.14). I didn't intend to slavishly follow them but I did want the cuts to have a definite, overall, radial appearance. A straightforward alternative would be tangential lines (see Fig 4.15), while curved and wavy lines and incomplete coverage of the surface are also

FIG 4.14 MARKING A FEW GUIDING LINES WITH A CENTRE-FINDER.

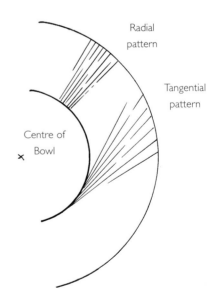

FIG 4.15 LINES CAN BE PLACED TANGENTIALLY; A SIMPLE JIG MAY HELP DRAW THE GUIDE LINES.

FIG 4.16 COMMENCING THE CUTS.
YOU MAY FIND THE TWO-HANDED
GRIP DISCUSSED IN CHAPTER 3 EASIER
ON HARDWOODS.

possibilities you could consider.

I would suggest you make practice cuts with the V tool on a spare piece of wood first, trying to get long strokes of uniform appearance.

Making sure the bowl was held securely, I simply started at one position and methodically worked my way around the rim in one direction, repositioning the bowl as necessary (see Figs 4.16 and 4.17). I kept the strokes long, but varied the starting and finishing points, and kept an eye on the drawn lines to make sure the direction was approximately right.

Make sure all your cuts are clean as you go along. When you have finished, check over the surface in a different light until you are happy with the quality of the effect.

Finishing

When all the decorating was complete, I took the bowl outside, away from the workshop and burnt the rim with a blow torch. I played the flame across the marks to bring them out, tending to make the inner and outer edges of the rim darker than the middle section. Putting the bowl back on the lathe I wiped the burned

FIG 4.17 NEARLY FINISHED. A
VARIETY OF GROOVES HAS BEEN
INTRODUCED AND THE BOWL FILLED
WITH LONG, CLEAN SHAVINGS.

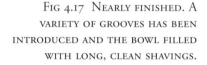

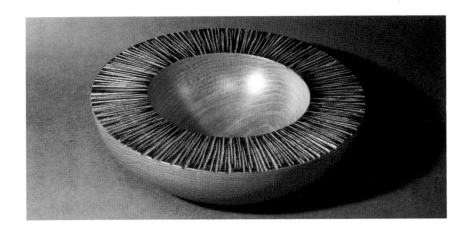

FIG 4.18 THE FINISHED BOWL, BURNT AND POLISHED.

surface with a coarse rag to remove surplus charcoal, fine sandpapered to smooth any sharp edges, and polished up the bowl with walnut oil (see Figs 4.18 and 4.19).

Originally I imagined the bowl, which is quite bold and coarse, full of smooth, shiny bonbons nestling unobtrusively (but handily) in a corner of the workshop. However, it has ended up full of bright, glassy marbles in the house. These do have the advantage of lasting longer, but are harder on the teeth.

FIG 4.19 DETAIL OF THE DECORATIVE MARKINGS CARVED IN BY THE V TOOL.

CHAPTER 5

Decorative marks II

WHEAT-EAR BREADBOARD

INTRODUCTION

FIG 5.1 THE PROJECT: A WHEAT-EAR BREADBOARD. A TRADITIONAL PIECE OF 'TREEN' (DOMESTIC WOODWARE) WITH DECORATIVE CARVING ENHANCING A PIECE OF PLAIN TURNING.

The project in this chapter will demonstrate how a design of simple but effective tool cuts can enhance an otherwise plain item of turning, as well as covering several more general points about carving technique (see Fig 5.1).

I will be making a very traditional piece of what is termed 'treen': wooden domestic ware such as that used in the past by poorer families who couldn't afford pewter. Treen includes bowls and platters, scoops and spoons, and in this case a breadboard. It was made locally and was probably the bread and butter of many a country turner. Local woods were used and simple carved patterns cut into each piece, more often than not by the users on a dark evening by the fireside.

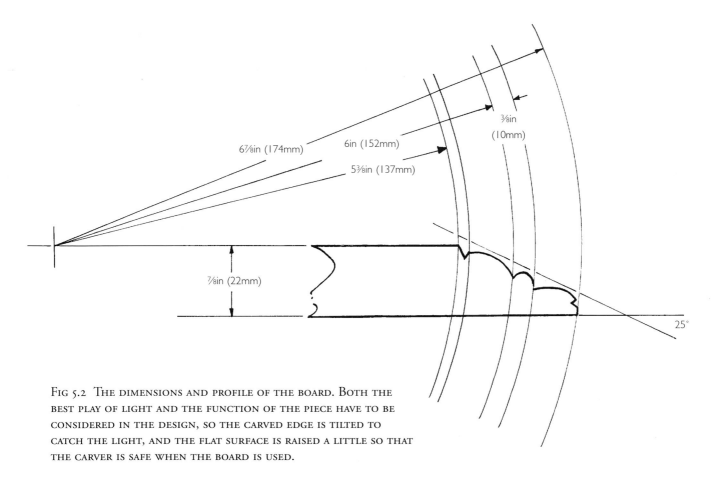

6⅞in (174mm)

6in (152mm)

5⅜in (137mm)

⅜in (10mm)

⅞in (22mm)

25°

FIG 5.2 THE DIMENSIONS AND PROFILE OF THE BOARD. BOTH THE
BEST PLAY OF LIGHT AND THE FUNCTION OF THE PIECE HAVE TO BE
CONSIDERED IN THE DESIGN, SO THE CARVED EDGE IS TILTED TO
CATCH THE LIGHT, AND THE FLAT SURFACE IS RAISED A LITTLE SO THAT
THE CARVER IS SAFE WHEN THE BOARD IS USED.

DESIGN

It is worth noting six key features of the design, as follows:

- In the profile shown in Fig 5.2 the carving itself is set along the edge of the board at an angle. This allows the light to catch and display the lines of the carving to their best advantage. Remember that the effect of light on a carving is always a prime consideration.
- The board is intended for use, for cutting on, so, to keep the bread knife from damaging the carved surface, the actual cutting area of the board is raised a little clear of the carving.
- The design is stylized; this is not really wheat but a carved representation of wheat. The carving tools cut a pleasing, repeating pattern suggesting the subject by means of simple representation (see Fig 5.3). This needs some thinking out first, and belongs to the type of work known as 'chip carving' – the chips of wood removed, in themselves, create the finished design; no modelling or sanding is required.

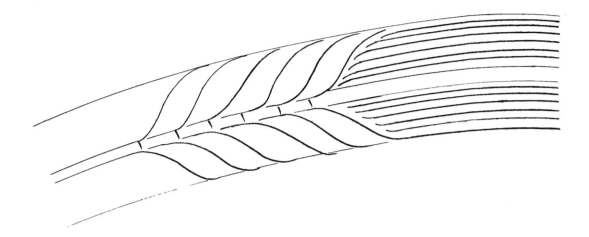

FIG 5.3 STYLIZING A DESIGN IS LIKE
RENDERING THE SUBJECT IN A
PLEASING SHORTHAND.

- The design also produces maximum effect in the shortest possible time. Carving wood takes a lot longer than turning it, and the labour cost is usually far higher than the material costs efficiency and effectiveness are therefore very important if the job is to be financially worthwhile. Along with this consideration, clean, slick cutting also gives a freshness to carved work and is a sign of confidence.

- The turned profile of the edge supports the carving. The main mass of the carved shape is the moulded edge as it comes off the lathe. It fits the tools I intend to use and the shapes I want to achieve. This is an example of another rule, common between carving and turning: always work the principal masses first and the detail will naturally fall into place.

- The ears of corn on the 'inside track' are smaller than those on the outside; the stem has not been placed in the true entre. This asymmetry adds a little more interest, as dead symmetry can be boring. Small changes can make major improvements to any piece of work and are always worth looking out for.

WOOD Any wood that you consider suitable for a plain, turned bread or chopping board will do: beech, sycamore or maple for example. I would suggest something mild and not too hard for your first attempt – I used a bit of Brazilian mahogany. A plain wood needs to be used to avoid camouflaging the actual carving – this is not to say the wood should have no figure, but any strong grain needs to be contained in the *centre* of the board. You could let in a different, more interesting wood (or even marble) into the centre for the cutting surface.

Project: Wheat-ear breadboard

Turning

The profile and dimensions of the board that I made are shown in Fig 5.2. Please note that the photograph of the board being turned on the lathe show a slightly different design to the board which is subsequently carved – an alternative which would give a slightly different appearance. However, I suggest you follow the drawn section as a first-off.

The breadboard is a standard piece of faceplate turning. The corner of the skew can be used to create the shadowy grooves (see Fig 5.4) and a small spindle gouge for the curves. Do not sand the area to be carved, but turn it cleanly – grit will damage the keen edges of carving tools. The working surface of the board and the very edge can be sanded however, and by all means do a little final sanding after carving is finished.

Divide the moulded edge with pencil marks into 16 parts: 8 for the ears and 8 for the stems and whiskers.

FIG 5.4 USING THE SKEW TO CREATE GROOVES.

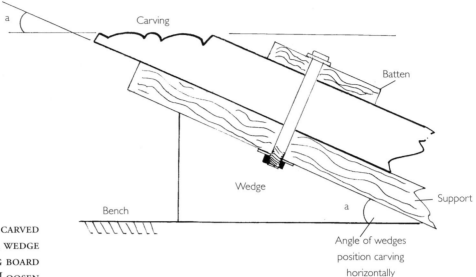

FIG 5.5 HOLDING THE CARVED HORIZONTAL USING A WEDGE BENEATH A SUPPORTING BOARD CLAMPED WITH A BATTEN. LOOSEN THE BOLTS, WHICH PASS TO EITHER SIDE, AND THE BOARD CAN BE ROTATED. THE BOARD IS, IN TURN, CLAMPED TO THE BENCH.

Holding the board

Once turned, the board can come off the lathe and on to a bench for carving; the lathe will not be needed again. Remember that the proper holding of any carving work involves:

- Keeping it absolutely still despite the effort of carving.
- Being able to get at the work safely and comfortably.
- Being able to reposition the work as easily as possible.

One option here is to clamp the board to the bench using a G clamp or bench holdfast. In practice the board needs to be gripped very tightly to stop it rotating. Another method would be to fix it with wedges, but here the bottom edge is a little tricky to get at.

If you're going to carve more than one board (and don't forget Christmas comes earlier every year) it is worth the effort to make a jig which sets the carved edge in a horizontal position. The breadboard is clamped with a cross-batten to a piece of wood which is then held at the appropriate angle using wedge-shaped offcuts. This is the method I used – it holds the workpiece safely, without it rotating, a quick turn of a spanner allowed it to be repositioned, and you can work along at least a third of the edge at any one time (see Fig 5.5).

Carving tools

This project involves only a few carving tools. Using the Sheffield list numbering the tools I used were:

> No. 6 x ⅜in (10mm) medium gouge for the inner cuts. I used a tapered tool, but a parallel-sided tool will do.
>
> No. 5 x ¼in (6mm) slightly flatter and narrower gouge; for the outer cuts.
>
> No. 8 x ³⁄₁₆in (5mm) small, quick gouge, nearly a half circle; for the nodes on the stem.
>
> No. 45 x ¼in (6mm) V tool, or similar size; for the whiskers.
>
> No. 2 x ⅜in (10mm) skew chisel, or similar size; for cleaning corners and the ends of the whiskers.

You may well find other suitable carving tools to carry out these tasks, hence avoiding any need to buy new ones especially for this job. Remember, a degree of interchangeability is a common practice in carving.

Carving

The edge is divided into 16 sections. A first section can be marked out to help line up the cutting edges of the gouges (see Fig 5.6). The sectional profile of the turned edge is a little different to the one shown in the photographs, but the appearance of the marking out would be just the same. I prefer to go straight into the cutting, positioning the carving tools by eye. The variation natural to handwork makes the board appear more warm and human. Don't worry if the spacings are not quite equal, or if you overshoot the end of a division, just cut in confidently and feel for the rhythm.

Carvers use one tool for as long as possible, to minimize down time. In this case, work around the whole edge with a gouge making one cut at a time. So you can take this approach of using a particular tool for as long as possible, and wherever possible, on the whole carving. Alternatively you may wish to complete a section of the carving at a time.

With the number 6 make a series of vertical stab cuts along the inner side of the stem, half-way across the width (see Fig 5.7). Hold the blade in the right hand like a pencil, while holding the handle in the left hand, like a dagger.

Join the vertical cuts with a second series of cuts at an angle – you should be able to ease out a series of crescent-shaped chips of wood

FIG 5.6

FIG 5.7

FIG 5.8

FIG 5.9.

FIG 5.10

FIG 5.11

FIG 5.6 MARKING OUT A FIRST SECTION TO BE SURE OF THE CUTS YOU HAVE IN MIND.

FIG 5.7 CUT THE FIRST 'INSIDE TRACK'.

FIG 5.8 A SECOND CUT AT AN ANGLE INTO THE FIRST REMOVES A CRESCENT-SHAPED CHIP OF WOOD.

FIG 5.9 THE FIRST CUT IN THE SECOND SERIES.

FIG 5.10 A SECOND CUT TO REMOVE A CRESCENT-SHAPED CHIP OF WOOD, BUT CURVING IN THE OPPOSITE DIRECTION TO THE PREVIOUS SERIES. THE GRAINS IN THE EAR TO ONE SIDE ARE NOW OBVIOUS.

FIG 5.11 THE NUMBER 8 GOUGE STARTS A SERIES OF ARCING CUTS TO MARK THE STEM BETWEEN THE EARS.

(see Fig 5.8). You will see that the angles at which the second cuts were made throw out little bevels of light.

Reverse the gouge to face the opposite way, and using first a vertical and then an angled cut, remove a second series of crescents, which merge with the first (see Figs 5.9 and 5.10). The seeds on the inside will now be delineated. Joining the two crescents requires a deft touch – go for clean crispness rather than neatness, using the skew to clean up any corners.

Repeat the procedure on the outer side of the wheat heads, using the number 5 – here the track is narrower than before. First cut one way round, then the other. You should now be able to see the wheat-ear.

Next, turn your attention to the stem within the ears of wheat. The smallest gouge, number 8, is used upside down to remove a series of cuts at points level with the wheat seeds (see Fig 5.11). Offer the gouge at about 30°, or even shallower, and lift the handle through an arcing cut, to end vertically (see Fig 5.12). This rounds the ends of the nodes. Use the point of the skew again to clean up the triangular recesses.

Now for the whiskers: use the V tool to create a series of parallel grooves (see Fig 5.13). Enter the cutting edge into the wood at about

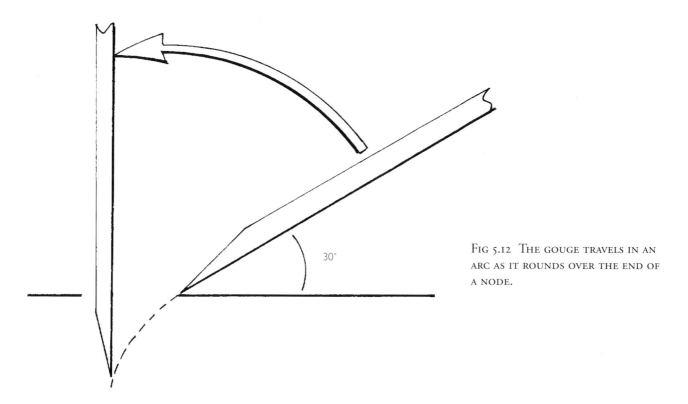

30°

FIG 5.12 THE GOUGE TRAVELS IN AN ARC AS IT ROUNDS OVER THE END OF A NODE.

35°, lower the handle to the proper cutting angle of about 20° and make a smooth, steady cut. Keep the hand wrapped around the blade and resting firmly on the wood at all times and use this hand as a brake to control the forward pressure of the pushing hand at the handle. I suggest the whisker lines come out of the end of the wheat-ear, but stop short of the next ear along. Clean up the ends with the point of the skew chisel (see Fig 5.14). Don't worry if they are not exactly parallel, they only need to *feel* right, as if they were rustling in the wind!

FIG 5.13 A V TOOL RUNS A SERIES OF PARALLEL GROOVES CREATING A 'BEARD' EFFECT.

FIG 5.14 USING THE CARVER'S SKEW CHISEL TO CLEAN UP THE ENDS OF THE V GROOVES.

FIG 5.13

FIG 5.14

FIG 5.15 DETAIL OF THE WHEAT-EAR
AFTER OILING AND POLISHING.

When the carving is finished, check over the board for any odd corner or recess that you may have missed, and tidy it up.

Finishing

A little edible oil, such as walnut, can be rubbed in, treating the board as you would any turning used for serving food. A vigorous rub with the shavings on the carving will polish it nicely (see Fig 5.15).

This simple sort of carving is essentially a surface decoration. It has many applications other than representing wheat-ears. For example, you could work crescent cuts and V grooves into mice for a cheese board or fish for a platter – or perhaps the cuts can be treated in a more abstract way to produce abstract, repeating patterns.

Lettering

CHAPTER 6

LETTERED BOWL

Lettering is one of those tasks that a turner may be asked to undertake, as many turned pieces, especially large plates and bowls, are given as commemorative items, for example at weddings or anniversaries. Indeed it may be that after working through this chapter, and building up your skill, you may like to offer lettering as a service.

Lettering is a beautiful craft in itself, with its own skills and disciplines. As such it has nothing to do with turning, and may be pursued independently of other forms of carving. The project in this chapter uses the turning as a vehicle for the lettering in a very conventional way, but there is scope for integrating the lettering with the object in a more artistic fashion.

Forms and families

To letter well, you must *understand* lettering; the families of shapes in any style of letter, the relationships between letters, words and sentences – in fact the whole work. This is an extremely important point and the main challenge. Lettering is unforgiving – it is hard to undo mistakes, and easy to spoil the work. You need to know what you are doing, and think each job through clearly.

First of all, *study* lettering. There are plenty of books on calligraphy and lettering styles in libraries, and even though these may deal with letters in ink, or carved in stone, the shapes and rhythms of the letters are universal and as such will be ideal to work from.

All the western styles of lettering find their roots in what is known as Trajan roman, named after Trajan's Column in Rome which is inscribed to what has long been accepted as an exquisite standard. It is a simplified version of this style that I will be using. From roman arose such styles as uncial and gothic. Anyone is free to modify letters to their heart's content – this is regularly done and has produced the thousands of commercial typefaces available today. Many styles are available in dry transfer letters, which can be used as patterns.

Laying out the letters

Bear in mind that the initial stage of drawing or laying out the letters may take as long as the carving – but it is on this stage that success depends, and it cannot be rushed.

When laying out letters aim for:

- Uniformity of 'colour'. This is the evenness with which letters are assembled and spaced – the balance between letters, within words, between words and so on. For example, putting two Ns together produces a tight effect between them – they need to be spaced a little wider apart (see Fig 6.1).
- Family features: what makes letters a 'style'; the root similarities and patterns between letters; the characteristic proportions, shapes and stresses (see Fig 6.2).

Carving letters is a slow process. In the example, the lettering took about three times as long as the initial turning of the bowl. I would strongly suggest that you practise your letters on a flat board first before going on to your carefully turned bowl; working on a curved surface is a little trickier than on a flat one. Besides reducing the risk of spoiling the turning, you can assess the size and type of tool that you need.

Fig 6.1 The importance of spacing between letters.

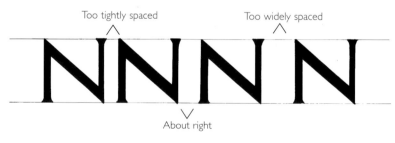

Fig 6.2 An instance of simple family resemblance: diagonals in one direction are thick, in the other, thin.

Project: Lettered bowl

Turning

The bowl I am using as an illustration was turned and carved in lacewood (London plane), around 18in (457mm) across and 5in (127mm) deep. It quotes the first line of Chapter 14 in the *Tao Tê Ching* by the Chinese philosopher Lao Tzu: 'Look, it cannot be seen – it is beyond form'. A wonderful saying for every turner to contemplate! The letters around the edge are about 1in (25mm) high (see Fig 6.3).

The bowl is an ordinary piece of turning. Although the grain is very busy in parts, its tight appearance does not interfere with the visibility of the letters – this is a very important consideration when choosing the type of wood to letter on. Don't sand the surface to be carved – it ruins the cutting edges of carving tools – but finish very smoothly with the bowl gouge or a similar tool. There is scope for final, judicious sanding when the work is finished off at the end.

Make sure the surface on which you carve is as flat as possible, otherwise you will have some tricky adjusting to prevent the letters appearing distorted. Working around the edge means the direction of grain changes, and sometimes the cutting is easier in some places than in others.

Make sure your carving tools are really sharp – I make no apologies for repeating this refrain. Never pull pieces out but cut everything crisply and cleanly. Use a stiff brush to clean out any dust.

Holding the bowl

I normally grip bowls and plates between two pieces of wood, cushioned with cork-lined pads of plywood. One of the pieces of wood is itself fixed to a swivel-ball hydraulic clamp – an extremely useful device which I use for all sorts of carving, and which in this case meant that I could position the bowl however I wanted. The only

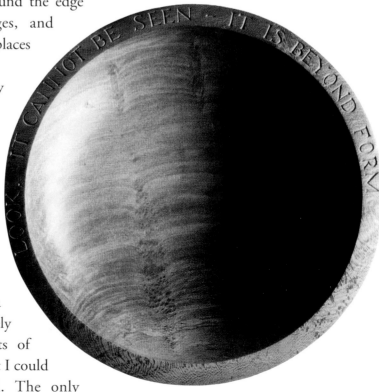

FIG 6.3 THE CARVED BOWL, NOW IN NORWAY, MADE FROM LACEWOOD (LONDON PLANE), 18IN (457MM) IN DIAMETER.

FIG 6.4 HOLDING THE BOWL IN ONE OF A LARGE RANGE OF POSITIONS USING THE ADJUSTABLE, SWIVEL BALL, SPENCER FRANKLIN HYDRACLAMP.

adjustment needed is to free the letters hidden under the batten at some convenient stage (see Fig 6.4). Without such a device you will need to arrange the bowl in a vice, or on the bench so that you can get at the letters easily.

Marking out

Always work out your letters on paper first. Calculate the length of line you have around the rim and the height of letters, then work out the width and proportions to give a pleasing arrangement. Decide where on the rim, in relation to the figure, you wish the letters to be placed.

With a circular bowl or plate it is best to take the centre of the bowl as the reference point in order to draw what would otherwise be vertical letters. This means that the letters actually taper slightly, making a logical sense in terms of the shape on which they are carved. The simplest way to mark them out is with a plastic centre-finder (see Fig 6.5). You can start at the centre of the calculated letters and work both ways. Try to make all your thick and thin lines of similar proportions as you go along.

Carving tools

You will need different tools for different sizes and styles of lettering. I suggest you learn and work with one size and style of letter until you are thoroughly familiar with the technique.

Chisels are needed for the straight elements – these need to be a little narrower than the total length to be cut, so as not to foul the serifs. You can make do with a narrower chisel by merging the cuts, but not a wider one. A skew chisel, or a small fishtail chisel should be used to clean the serif ends.

Gouges cut the curves, and fewer are needed than you might think. One gouge will take its sweep from the radius of the largest curves and will be used to cut the outside of the letters. Another, flatter, gouge is used to cut the inside curves. A small, flat, fishtail gouge is ideal for the serifs.

Carving

Let us look at how I carved five letters: two straight, A and N; and three with curves, C, B and S. Some basic principles will be apparent which will apply to other letters with similar features. Look carefully at the way I hold the tools to make the cuts.

To carve A and N, start with the thicker 'leg' of the letter. Push

FIG 6.5 MARKING OUT THE 'VERTICALS' WITH A CENTRE FINDER.

FIG 6.6

FIG 6.7

FIG 6.8

FIG 6.6 AN INITIAL STOP CUT TO THE
LETTER A.

FIG 6.7 DEFINING THE APEX WITH
THE CORNER OF THE CHISEL.

FIG 6.8 USING A SHALLOW FISHTAIL
TO FORM THE SERIF.

the chisel vertically in the centre, stopping short of each end – the
serif goes here. This is a *stop cut* (see Fig 6.6). Stop cuts are important
for most letters; they prevent the fibres from tearing or popping out
beyond where the cutting edge is entering.

Take out the left and right sides of the leg with a cut from each
direction, angled down to join at the centre line and create a V-shaped
trench. Try to work neatly from your surface lines, producing a clean
junction at the bottom and using one cut for each side if possible.

Make a diagonal stop cut into the apex of the A, then make a
central stop cut in the thinner leg as before and remove the wood in
two cuts, cleaning up the apex with the corner of the chisel (see Fig
6.7). Remember, this leg must be shallower than the thicker leg.

Use the corner of the fishtail gouge and skew chisel to form the serif

FIG 6.9 CLOSE-UP OF SOME OF THE
LETTERS SHOWING THE A.

on either end to the bottom line (see Fig 6.8). Note that the shape of
the serif is not the same on each side – this is very often the case, and
is something you will discover when you research the shapes!

It now only remains to put in the horizontal bar, making the usual
stop cut first, and the letter A is finished (see Fig 6.9). You can use
this pattern of cutting for all straight letters: E, F, H, I, K, L, M, N,
T, V, W, X, Y and Z. Fig 6.10 shows the same sequence of central
stop cuts, stop cuts into the corners, cutting in the sides and forming
the serifs used in the carving of the N.

There are straight elements in some other letters: B, D, G, J, P, R
and U (see Fig 6.11). When you come to these, remember to try and
merge straight and curved parts together.

Let us now move on to cutting curves, using B, C and S as
examples. The curved elements of letters usually give beginners a
little more trouble than the straight parts, but they are far more fun
and satisfying once you know how to cut them. The secret is to
sweep the edge of the gouge round in a controlled, slicing action,
tilted to allow the corner to do a lot of the work, and cut out a
crescent, or a series of merging crescents. Hold the tool like a pencil
in one hand and swing the handle round with the other.

Start with a central, vertical stop cut as before. Fig 6.12 shows this,
followed by a suitably curved gouge sweeping around the outside of
this central stop cut in the letter C.

This cut is followed by one to the inside using a flatter tool. The
first (stop cut) gouge is used to make a similar sweeping cut to the
outside of the letter, but you can take these cuts in either order. Both
outside and inside cuts must angle in towards the centre line and meet
neatly to remove the woodchip (see Fig 6.13). You may have to clean
up the bottom of the crescent a little using the corner of the gouge.

In the letter B, cut the vertical stem first. Fig 6.14 shows the lower

FIG 6.11

FIG 6.12

FIG 6.13

FIG 6.14

FIG 6.15

FIG 6.16

FIG 6.11 CLOSE-UP OF SOME OF THE LETTERS SHOWING THE D.

FIG 6.12 THE FIRST STAGE IS ALWAYS THE STABBING IN OF A CENTRE STOP CUT. MORE THAN ONE GOUGE MAY BE NEEDED TO FOLLOW THE VARYING SHAPE OF A CURVED LETTER.

FIG 6.13 THE CUTTING EDGE IS SWEPT AROUND THE LETTER SHAPE, AND CUTS ARE MERGED TO FORM CLEAN LINES.

FIG 6.14 ON THE LETTER B, THE BOTTOM CURVE DIFFERS DISTINCTLY FROM THE TOP AND DIFFERENT TOOLS WILL BE NEEDED. THIS IS WHERE RESEARCH IS IMPORTANT.

FIG 6.15 CLOSE-UP OF SOME OF THE LETTERS, SHOWING THE S.

FIG 6.16 MAKING THE SERIFS IN THE LETTER S WITH THE SKEW CHISEL.

curved part being removed in a similar fashion to the C. You will of course need different sizes of tools for the upper and lower curves. The serifs are nicked in, as for the A.

S is the letter that intimidates people. The best approach is to regard the shape as two simple, reversed curves and take each carefully in turn (see Fig 6.15), making sure you have drawn it well. In the style I used, I made a small flat central section first, into which I merged the ends of the upper and lower curves. The flat section simplifies the business of bringing the two curves together neatly. If the style does not include a flat section, then merging the upper and lower curves becomes a little trickier, and you may find a skew chisel is the best tool to use (see Fig 6.16).

Other curved letters that use this tool technique include D, G, J, O, P, R, U.

Finishing

Clean off the drawing marks with fine sandpaper on a block. Brush well and change the lighting to see if any touching up is needed.

Lettering can be a full-time craft, but I hope this chapter has inspired you to explore the field further.

Low relief I

CHAPTER 7

MILKING STOOL

This milking stool, a birthday present for a little boy keen on nursery rhymes, gives me the opportunity to talk about and demonstrate what is known as *relief carving* (see Figs 7.1 and 7.2).

Relief carving defines any carved work where the subject features against a reduced background. Varying levels or planes within a main outline are 'relieved' against each other to give an illusion of greater three-dimensionality than is really present. The main point is that the subject is still attached to the background (or simply 'the ground' as carvers refer to it). The extent to which the background is taken down can be slight ('low relief') or very deep ('high relief'). In between is 'medium relief', but the borderline between these terms is very indistinct.

The ground itself needn't be flat – such as a panel, or in this project – but can be part of a curved surface such as a bowl or vase. As with everything else demonstrated in this book, I want to emphasize the point that the techniques of relief carving, once mastered, have endless applications.

Let us look first at a few key points about low relief work. First, low relief carving is not far short of two-dimensional, reducing the background only enough to make the design stand out a little. This means that the design *as a drawing* is important. Second, it is the *outline* of the design which is most distinct. The outline should be readily recognizable and well cut. The whole work will, by its nature, be *flat*, with little depth to the changes of plane, and with the possibility of only light modelling (see Fig 7.3). In the case of the milking stool I also stained the background to emphasize the silhouette even more.

Finally, it is generally considered bad carving practice to

INTRODUCTION

FIG 7.1 TOP VIEW OF THE FINISHED STOOL SHOWING THE DETAILS OF THE CARVING.

FIG 7.2 THE FINISHED STOOL.

carve horizontal surfaces! One reason is that they collect dust. Another is that these are surfaces on which objects are placed, although chip carving – where a large amount of the original surface level remains – is an exception. In this case, however, I've made another exception. I reasoned that as the only object to be placed on the stool would be a little boy's bottom, this bottom would no doubt balance well enough. As for dust, I expected the trousers to do the polishing. In the end the carving was low enough not to be felt, which was even more important. So in this case it worked – but do keep the carving light, and always bear in mind the function of the piece on which you are working.

FIG 7.3 A CROSS-SECTION THROUGH A LOW RELIEF CARVING. NOTE THAT THE DISTANCE BETWEEN THE OUTSIDE (PROFILE) OF THE SUBJECT AND THE BACKGROUND IS GREATER THAN ANY CHANGES OF PLANE WITHIN THE SUBJECT. MOST OF THE SURFACE IS FLAT WITH ONLY THE EDGES AND DEFINING LINES MODELLED.

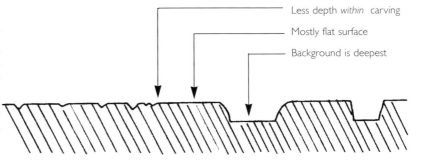

Less depth *within* carving

Mostly flat surface

Background is deepest

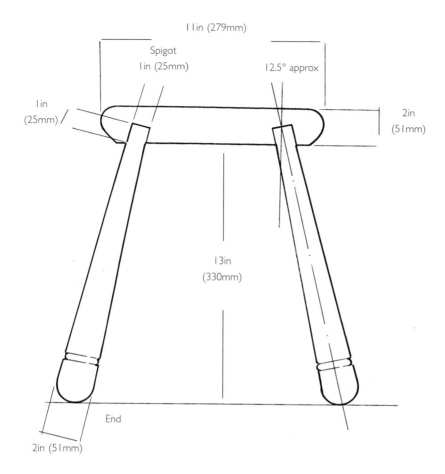

11in (279mm)

Spigot
1in (25mm)

12.5° approx

1in
(25mm)

2in
(51mm)

13in
(330mm)

End

2in (51mm)

DESIGN

I made the stool in the classic three-legged design which sits comfortably on a rough barn floor (see Fig 7.4). The top had to be thick to take the spigots of the legs, which made it appear heavy, so I 'weighted' the legs by splaying the wood towards the ground and adding a coloured ring to echo the stain I used on the top.

It is very important to note that the feet of the stool lie *outside* the diameter of the seat. For this an angle of 10–15° (max) is needed. If you make another size of stool, do a full-size drawing first to work out an angle sufficient for stability, but not great enough to weaken the joint.

I rounded the top edge of the stool for comfort, continuing the line in and under the stool, opposing the splay of the legs and making a pleasing balance. I also rounded over the feet; you could saw them off flush to the floor, but I'm for the easy life!

The joints themselves are those at which turners excel: a spigot inserted into a bored hole. Make them a tight fit. A really nice touch would be to secretly wedge the end of the spigot – a 'foxed' tenon.

The drawing was worked out so that the back of the moon could

x = Centre of
circle diam
8⅝in (220mm)

Section

FIG 7.5 THE DESIGN; A PHOTOCOPIER
WAS USED TO ENLARGE IT TO THE SIZE
REQUIRED.

be precisely turned, and would give me a starting depth. The feet of the cow also come on to the line of the circle. The star fills in what would otherwise be a recess, and was a request, since 'Twinkle, Twinkle' ranks as my customer's second favourite nursery rhyme. If you want to use my design, remember photocopiers as really quick ways to get a drawing to the size you want (see Fig 7.5).

WOOD

The wood I used was mahogany, salvaged from a liquidated joinery firm. Other plain wood such as light-coloured sycamore or maple would look very good. Something tight-grained which will take fine detail, and bland so that the design is not obscured by the grain. Start with a clean, planed piece of wood, preferably not sanded on the side you want to carve. When you bandsaw the disc, keep the concave offcuts to clamp the seat to the bench for carving.

Project: Milking stool

Turning

The top is simple faceplate turning. A trick worth mentioning – and which is very useful if you ever want to make a lot of three-legged stools, carved or otherwise – is that I altered the faceplate to have three holes set exactly 120° apart and a set distance from the centre. These holes, through which I screwed the plate to the wood, accurately mark the position of the legs. When the leg holes are bored, the faceplate screw holes – which might otherwise remain visible – are removed. This saves a lot of time but does need a little thinking through as to the size of stool seat and so on.

1in (25mm) screws were enough to fix the faceplate to the wood. I rounded over the edge with a sharp bowl gouge and, with a small parting tool, took the rebate around the moon to the required depth (see Fig 7.6). The background depth of the low relief carving should be less than ⅛in (3mm), so this should be the depth of the cut – otherwise someone's bottom will be imprinted with the design when they stand up!

Bore the holes on a pillar drill for greatest accuracy of angle. I used a 1in (25mm) Forstner bit.

The legs are basic spindle turning. Work the spigots first – this is

FIG 7.6 A PARTING TOOL USED AS A
SCRAPER TO LET IN THE OUTSIDE
EDGE OF THE GROUND, BEHIND THE
MOON. THE DEPTH I SET HERE WAS
THE SAME FOR THE OVERALL CARVING.

FIG 7.7 THE SPIGOT WAS MADE AN ACCURATE FIT FIRST, THEN THE LEG NICELY TAPERED TO MERGE INTO IT. NO SHOULDER WAS LEFT – WHICH WOULD NEED CUTTING AT AN ANGLE.

the most important part to get right. Make them a 'fat' 1in (25mm) to fit the holes in the seat; you can always sand them a bit by hand to get a good fit. Use a roughing gouge to get the taper of the leg, smoothing the line imperceptibly into the spigot, finishing and cutting the beads with a skew (see Fig 7.7). Sand well. Any finish can be applied on the lathe, but keep the spigots bare for the glue.

Carving tools

The tools I used in this project were (using the Sheffield list):

Nos 1, 4 and 6 x ½in (13mm).
Nos 3, 6, 9 and V tool x ¼in (6mm).
Nos 3 and 7 x ⅛in (3mm).

All the tools were straight.

You will see in some of the photographs how I used G clamps and pieces of the circular offcuts to hold the seat in place on the bench.

Carving

The first stage consists of 'setting in' the outline to the drawing and removing the background. The second stage is the subsequent work *within* the outline – delineating any planes and adding some light modelling.

Trace or carbon paper the design on the top, lining up the grain to go through the weakest parts of the design, such as the cow's horns.

Start with the V tool and, without being a slave to the line, run a groove around the outline – on the waste side of the line, but up *to* the line. If you do this neatly, with a flowing line and to the depth of the background, then that line becomes the edge of the silhouette.

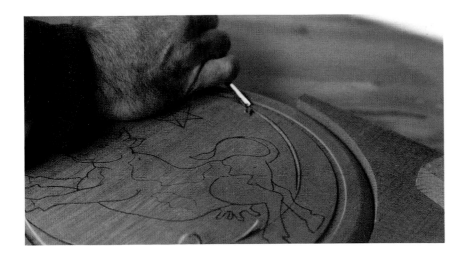

FIG 7.8 THE DRAWING WAS APPLIED
WITH CARBON PAPER AND THE STOOL
TOP HELD WITH OFFCUTS FROM THE
ORIGINAL BANDSAWING. HERE I
STARTED OUTLINING THE FORMS WITH
THE V TOOL. REMEMBER TO MAKE
THE LINES FLOW AND MAINTAIN A
CONSTANT DEPTH.

Do make an effort to cut as precisely with the V tool as you can –
this is the secret of an efficient low relief carving (see Fig 7.8). You
will also appreciate the need for real sharpness here!

Three points:

- Whenever the V tool is cutting diagonally to the grain, one side
  of the V will be with the grain, the other against it. Working on
  the waste side, cut so that the direction of the tool leaves a clean
  cut (i.e. with the grain) on the carving   side (see Fig 7.9).
- Never run the V tool off unsupported ends, such as the tips of
  the moon, the points of the star, or the horns. Cut *into* the
  mass where the fibres are supported and will not tear away.
- Where the detail is too complicated for the simple strokes of
  the V tool, work as near as you can but leave blocks of outline
  – e.g. between the ears – to be set in with differently shaped
  gouges (see Fig 7.10).

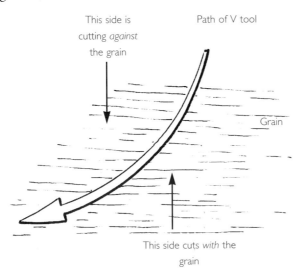

This side is
cutting *against*
the grain

Path of V tool

Grain

This side cuts *with* the
grain

FIG 7.9 CUT WITH THE V TOOL SO
THAT THE SIDE CUTTING WITH THE
GRAIN IS TO THE CARVING. THIS MAY
MEAN REVERSING THE TOOL AND
CUTTING FROM THE OPPOSITE
DIRECTION.

FIG 7.10 MAIN OUTLINE COMPLETED WITH THE PARTING TOOL. NOTE THE 'ABBREVIATION' AROUND THE HORNS, HEAD AND UDDERS, ENABLING ME TO REMOVE THE GROUND AS QUICKLY AS POSSIBLE AND SET IN THESE MORE COMPLICATED AREAS LATER.

FIG 7.11 RELIEVING THE GROUND USING A FLATTER GOUGE.

Having outlined the main drawing, lightly remove the background with the medium gouge (number 6). Finish off the background surface with the flatter gouges (numbers 3 or 4 – see Fig 7.11). Remember, the 'depth' is shallow so this should be a quick process.

Set in the detail using differently shaped gouges, offering them to the wood at the same angle as the edge cut by the V tool – this slightly sloping edge to the wood catches the light and is stronger than a vertical edge. The idea is to neatly marry the walls of the carving with the background, not leaving stab or score lines (see Fig 7.12). The background need not be truly flat, but should *appear* so. Use the ⅛in (3mm) tools for the tricky bits (see Fig 7.13) and don't forget the useful skew chisel for the corners.

When the main outline is neat and tidy, with the background clean and level without tears, the internal relief modelling can begin. Start by separating the legs and udders from the body and the head from the neck using the V tool, going to about half the depth of the outline. Then merge in the forms. Remember this is a flat piece of work, so only float in the edges, leaving the main work flat (see Fig 7.14).

Outlining with simple cuts is required where the hind legs overlap the moon. Don't take too much away from the moon. Vulnerable ends, such as the tips, need taking down more towards the background to prevent them being broken off.

Modelling involves a few tool cuts and strokes only; there is little opportunity for elaboration, so make each cut tell.

The track of the star was designed to complement and balance the curve of the moon. Reduce the thickness of the track so that, from a full depth at the star, it is at the level of the background when it reaches the edge of the design. Then use the V tool to run its descriptive lines. These need not be equally spaced, but they do need to curve smoothly away.

Soften the outline of the main silhouette, rounding it over with an inverted gouge. Now is a good time for a final check: torn fibres, whiskers and stab marks should all be cleaned up and lines all made true.

Finally I used a frosting tool to stipple the cow, suggesting black and white markings. At the same time I frosted some of the background to 'lift' the forms a little – do this sparingly and meaningfully, leaving plenty of empty space.

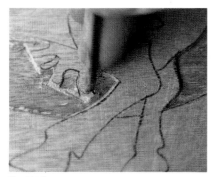

FIG 7.12

FIG 7.13

FIG 7.14

Finishing

After gluing the legs in position, I sealed the wood with a coat of polyurethane varnish and then coloured the background with a ('mahogany'!) varnish stain. I did this because, as I have mentioned before, carving depends for its effects on light and shadow, and being low relief, light from above tends to fall evenly across the surface, leaving very little shadow and making the features difficult to see. This may well be a third reason why carving is mostly preferred on vertical surfaces. It also brings out my point about the importance of the silhouette.

I applied a final coat of polyurethane to finish. I am not a fan of varnish, but in this case I expected the stool to get rough, if not messy, treatment – and not in the cowshed either!

Low relief carving is essentially a decorative surface finish, and turned work presents many surfaces which are suitable for this technique. It *does* ask for some drawing ability, but there are many books and illustrations which can be used as starting points.

FIG 7.12 'SETTING IN' DETAILS OF THE OUTLINE WITH APPROPRIATELY SHAPED GOUGES.

FIG 7.13 CUT IN NEATLY TO THE RIGHT DEPTH.

FIG 7.14 WHEN THE BACKGROUND IS FINISHED, THE INTERNAL SEPARATION OF PLANES WITH THE V TOOL CAN BEGIN, FOLLOWED BY LIGHT MODELLING OF THE INTERNAL SURFACES. KEEP MOST OF THE CARVING FLAT.

CHAPTER 8

Low relief II

FOUR-POSTER
BEDPOST VASE

INTRODUCTION

In the last chapter I looked at some of the techniques involved in a piece of simple, low relief carving. Now I will take these techniques a little further and look at one well-established area in which carving and turning have been combined: the four-poster bed. It may appear a more ambitious project, but careful scrutiny will show you that the work is essentially what I did on the stool – only more of it.

Originally the four posts were part of a structure that was draped with fabric to form an enclosed space. The first four-posters were probably placed in the corner of the room with posts up to the ceiling, only one side and the foot end being draped. The idea was to sleep in a snug sort of Wendy house, sealed from the cold draughts circulating through the rest of the home. The next stage was for the bedposts to become free-standing, with the mattress platform moving in or out of the structure.

For wealthy Elizabethans such beds became huge oak contraptions with the bed integral to the posts. The Georgians refined them using the newly-acquired mahoganies. The Victorians poured on the decoration, making them heavy-looking again. Finally, after Art Nouveau, new designs for turned and carved bedposts dried up when simpler, more functional styles came into fashion. Today, most customers want reproductions of past glories, and it is often to the turner rather than the carver that they go first.

I will only be looking at the carved part of the post in this chapter, but these details – together with many of the other techniques with which I have been dealing – apply to a wide variety of styles.

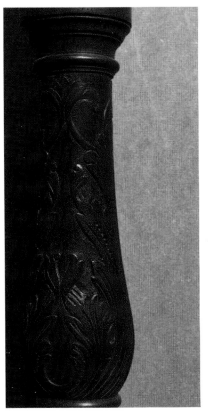

FIG 8.1 THE VASE OF THE BEDPOST, DATED AROUND 1790.

FOUR-POSTER
BEDPOSTS

I worked with a reproduction in mahogany of a post dated about 1790 (see Fig 8.1). Most four-posters have two plain, square posts at the head end, which are hidden behind drapes, and two foot posts –

the visible, decorated ones. Usually these ornamented posts have four parts (see Fig 8.2):

- A base block to which the mattress frame, the head and the footboards will be attached. Such a block may have applied carvings or a ball and claw foot.
- A 'vase' or decorated urn section. This is often turned as part of the block, but it may be separate and fitted to the block with a hefty spigot.
- The 'post' proper. Sometimes octagonal, but mostly turned. To make subsequent fluting, reeding or barley-twisting easier, the post is usually turned as a unit on its own and spigoted to the vase at the lower end and the capital at the top.
- A top piece or 'capital'. Again, often turned separately from the post, allowing the ends of the fluting or reeding to be finished off. It may be carved with leaves, for example, and also takes the canopy apron or cornice.

So there could be three or four separate pieces of wood to turn or carve: the block, the vase, the post (fluted or reeded), and the top capital. This has the advantage of a more economic use of wood, and ease of handling and working. Additionally, not many turners have lathes to take the total length.

In this chapter I will only be looking at the turning and carving of the vase part of the bedpost. Although the carving of only one post is described, you would of course be making a pair, and before embarking on a project such as this, it is important to do some research. There are books on the subject in libraries, and museums with many examples on display. You need to have a clear idea of what you are doing, what sizes are involved, how you will proceed and so on – I strongly advise you *not* to make the design up as you go along. Next, make a full size drawing of the turning profile, and one of the carving design (see Fig 8.3). Regard the design as flat, then wrapped around the turning.

FIG 8.2 THE BASIC PARTS OF A TYPICAL FOUR-POSTER BEDPOST.

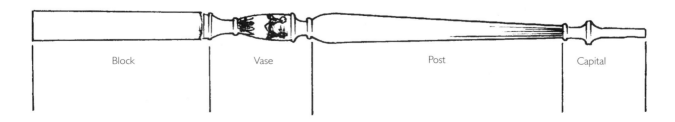

| Block | Vase | Post | Capital |

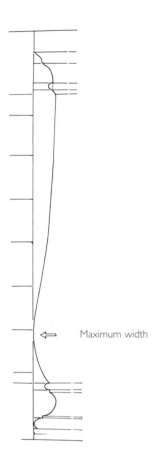

Maximum width

FIG 8.3 THE PROFILE OF THE WORKED
VASE. A WOODEN VERSION OF THIS
PATTERN WOULD BE USED IN THE
NORMAL FASHION TO REPEAT THE
DESIGN BETWEEN POSTS.

FIG 8.4 TURNING THE VASE.

Project: Four-poster bedpost vase

Turning

This is straightforward between-centres work and should not present too many problems (see Fig 8.4). Try and match the pair of posts as accurately as you can. If they do end up a little different, this is not normally a problem. Being spaced so far apart, they will not be examined simultaneously. On posts of this period the turning is often very detailed and you should pay attention to getting this right. The vase shapes are elegant and you need to feel for the lines. Bore the holes and match the spigots early. Make the spigot a third of the diameter of the block of wood into which it will insert, and a minimum length of 2in (51mm), which implies a first class fit. 4in (102mm) is better.

Remember, it is unwise to sand any part of a turning which is to be carved, as it affects the finely sharpened edges of the carving tools.

There is a small part of the turning where you can reduce the diameter to the background (see Fig 8.5); always take advantage of an opportunity to set levels with the turning.

After the turning is complete, disconnect the lathe so that there is no danger of turning it on accidentally.

Marking out

The working drawing is now applied to the vase (see Figs 8.5 and 8.6). Unlike the previous chapter, you cannot successfully use carbon paper. The best way is to divide the drawing into squares – the same technique which is used for the barley twist in Chapter 11.

I used four lines to quarter the length; the drawing shows the placing of the cylindrical lines that I used. The trick here is to find a division that touches important intersecting lines in the drawing.

The carving on this bedpost is 'handed': there is a left and right direction to the top leaves. Most of the drawing must still be placed by eye (see Fig 8.7).

Lock the lathe and copy the drawing on to the vase. As you see I use a Harrison Graduate, the crude locking of which entails a spanner applied to the mandrel. I find that a simple wooden wedge

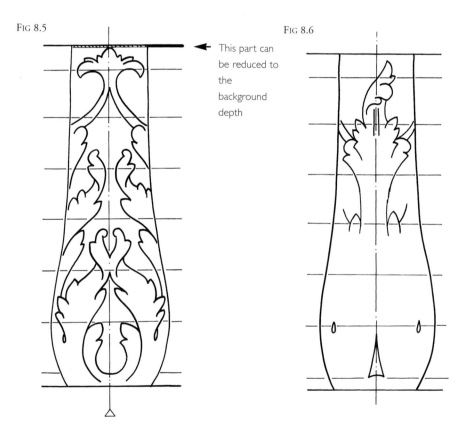

Fig 8.5

Fig 8.6

◄— This part can be reduced to the background depth

FIG 8.5 DETAILED DRAWINGS ARE NECESSARY FOR THIS SORT OF WORK – BUT ONLY THE OUTLINES. DIVIDE THE DRAWING UP TO HELP IN TRANSFERRING IT TO THE TURNED WOOD. NOTE WHERE THE DIAMETER CAN BE REDUCED TO THE BACKGROUND.

FIG 8.6 A VIEW AT 90° TO FIG 8.5. AGAIN, ALL THE VEINING DETAILS CAN BE LEFT OUT, AND ONLY THE PRINCIPLE POINTS HAVE BEEN MARKED.

FIG 8.7 DRAWING OUT THE DESIGN
ON TO THE TURNING IS LARGELY
ACHIEVED 'BY EYE', USING A GRID
SYSTEM FOR REFERENCE – THE
GUIDING LINES ARE CLEARLY VISIBLE.

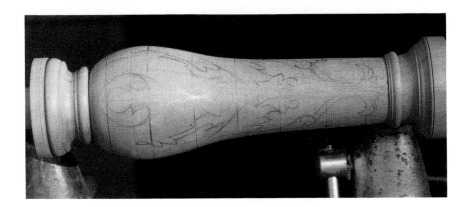

between spindle pulley and casing is quite adequate to stop the work revolving.

Clamp a board on to the lathe bed to take your carving tools. Note in Fig 8.8 how they are lined up nicely – this protects them from damaging their edges and allows them to be discerned more easily.

Carving tools

The carving tools I used in this project were:

Nos 3, 6 and V tool x ¼in (6mm).
Nos 3, 9 and 11 (veiner) x ⅛in (3mm).
Skew chisel.
Odd tools to match shapes where necessary.

All the tools were straight.

FIG 8.8 CLAMP A PLATFORM TO THE
BED OF THE LATHE TO HOLD THE
CARVING TOOLS. START BY OUTLINING
THE DESIGN WITH A SMALL V TOOL,
KEEPING TO THE WASTE SIDE OF ALL
LINES.

Carving

The first stage of relief carving is the outlining. Run a V tool around the waste side of the leaf edges, to a depth of ¼6in (2mm) or thereabouts – this is *low* relief, and you should find it quite quick. Try and make the grooves smooth, uniform and flowing.

After you have outlined as much with the V tool as you can, use different gouges to 'set in' the remaining leaf shapes. For example the large circular junction between two sets of leaves can be struck with the correct sweep of gouge (see Fig 8.9).

By all means adapt the design to the carving tools you have available, but remember what you use so that you can repeat the effect on the second post.

The next stage, as with the pattern, is the 'grounding'. This means removing ('relieving') waste wood around the principal design to the required background level. In this case the depth is very shallow, so you can proceed straight to the flattest (number 3) gouges. In addition to the ¼in and ⅛in (number 6 and number 3) gouges, you may find you need something really small – ¼6in (2mm) for example (see Fig 8.10).

Use the point of the carver's skew to clean up difficult corners (see Fig 8.11). Work neatly up to the edges of the outlining and setting in – don't leave stab marks or tears. Carve this way methodically over the whole of the vase.

Remember to keep to the circular quality of the turning surface

FIG 8.9 USING A GOUGE WITH THE RIGHT SWEEP TO SET IN THE CURVED JUNCTION BETWEEN LEAF SETS.

FIG 8.10 USING A SMALL FLAT GOUGE TO RELIEVE THE BACKGROUND. REMEMBER TO FOLLOW THE CURVING SURFACE OF THE TURNING.

FIG 8.11 THE SKEW CHISEL WILL CLEAN THOSE CORNERS WHICH OTHER TOOLS WILL NOT REACH.

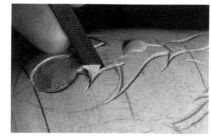

FIG 8.10

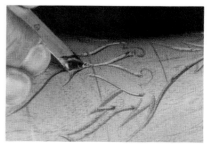

FIG 8.11

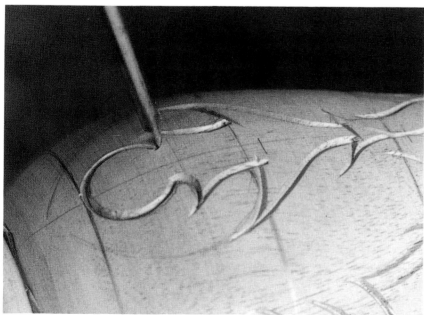

FIG 8.9

FIG 8.12 SEPARATING LEAVES WITHIN THE OVERALL PROFILE OF THE CARVING.

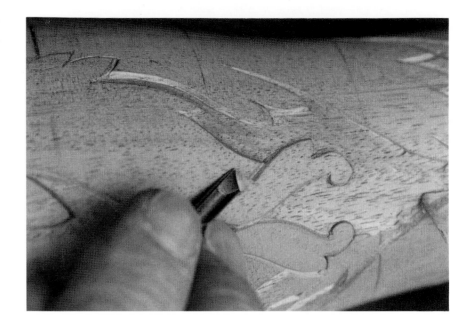

and do not carve a series of flat facets. Where possible throughout the carving, work 'downhill', from the greatest diameter (the bulge in the vase) to the smaller, in the same way you would if you were turning.

If you want to make the background even smoother, you can work a small scraper, made from an old hacksaw blade, evenly *with* the grain. Feel free to reverse the wood between centres.

When the whole of the foliage profile has been set in and the background relieved and finished, the next (and perhaps more interesting) stage of modelling can begin.

Start by using the V tool and flat gouges to separate the leaves *within* the profile. Run the surface of what is now a secondary ground smoothly up to the edges of the leaves, leaving them proud (see Fig 8.12). The depth can be the 1/16in (2mm) that was used before *within* the leaf design, but as you get to the true outside edges, reduce this to allow a full depth of primary background.

Do not undercut any of the design – bedposts tend to be handled and there is a danger of clothes catching on projecting points. It is worth emphasizing that you should always consider how, and in what context, your work will be used.

'Eyes', where leaf bases join, are cut with a small semicircular (number 9) gouge first and the leaves separated into the characteristic 'eye' shape. As such eyes are usually quite small, these correspondingly small number 9s are sometimes called 'eye tools'.

The one I used is about ⅛in (3mm). Offer the tool vertically to the surface of the wood where you want the body of the eye to be and wind it around so that it cuts a neat circle. As it cuts deeper you should find that the little circle of wood breaks off and pops out under the wedge-like pressure of the bevel. You then need to merge the edges of the hole into the edges of the leaves, forming the characteristic eye shape (see Fig 8.13).

Use an 'eye punch' (in fact a large nail, shaped on the grinder) to flatten the bottom. The base of the punch is flat and the sides taper slightly, preventing it from getting stuck in the hole. When the punch is tapped into the eye, the bottom of the eye is flattened and deepened, giving it more shadow and therefore more flair (see Fig 8.14).

There is a triangular facet filling the space between the two sweeping bands of leaves. This is cut by pushing the point of the skew chisel from deep in the centre of the triangle to the surface at the corners. This is a 'stop cut', frequently used in chip carving and lettering (see Chapter 6). Do not wobble the skew from side to side, as there is a danger of snapping off the buried corner. A small fishtail chisel is ideal for removing the waste, but the skew itself or the flat gouges can also be used for this.

Once all the leaves within the profile of the carving have been separated, the design will have begun to emerge and make sense. It is very important that a simple layout and flow of leaves is readily recognizable before you begin to carve the complex veins and surface decoration.

What happens next is a bit of magic – what is actually simple will now appear complicated – and impressive. Figs 8.15 and 8.16 show the veining of the leaves in detail. Use small U-shaped tools (number 10 or 11) or the V tool if you have nothing else, to run grooves in a similar way as in the outlining stage. Make these logical with respect to the underlying pattern of the leaves, which should sweep and unfold naturally. Think of it as free-hand drawing.

I enjoy this stage more than any other part of the carving. Work with the grain where possible. Remember that this is *handwork* and there is bound to be variation and inequality – keep the feel and appearance of the whole piece in mind as you work.

Crescent-shaped cuts and rows of point punch marks are also characteristic of this sort of work.

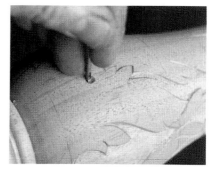

FIG 8.13 SETTING IN THE 'EYE' BETWEEN TWO LEAVES WITH A SMALL NUMBER 9. LET THE EDGE ROTATE AND CUT ITS OWN CIRCLE – THE WASTE BIT IN THE MIDDLE WILL POP OUT. ANOTHER SMALL GOUGE IS THEN NEEDED TO SHAPE THE EYE PROPER.

FIG 8.14 AN EYE PUNCH WILL FLATTEN, DEEPEN AND CLEAN THE BOTTOM OF THE EYE.

FIG 8.15

FIG 8.16

FIG 8.15 DETAILS OF THE SURFACE
MODELLING. LONG LINES IN THIS
PART OF THE CARVING ARE CARVED BY
EYE, ALTHOUGH YOU MAY LIKE TO
DRAW IN SOME TO START OFF WITH IN
PENCIL. NOTE THE SHORT STROKES
TO INDIVIDUAL LEAVES. THE
BACKGROUND DOES NOT HAVE TO BE
ABSOLUTELY FLAT, ONLY FEEL FLAT.
THE SELECTIVELY-PLACED ROW OF
POINT PUNCH MARKS ADDS A LITTLE
MORE INTEREST.

FIG 8.16 MORE DETAILS OF THE
SURFACE MODELLING. NOTE THE
CRESCENT CUTS TO THE LEAF FOLD
AND THE DEEP TRIANGULAR CUT,
PRODUCED MAINLY WITH THE SKEW
CHISEL. IT IS SURPRISING HOW
COMPLICATED THE SIMPLE VEINING
STROKES MAKE THE FINAL
APPEARANCE.

Finishing

After all the veining and detailing is completed, carefully examine the work, in different lights if possible, for torn grain or anything else that could be tidied up.

Remember, the carving on bedposts like this will be handled, so it must *feel* pleasing, without any sharp corners. To this end take some very fine sandpaper (say 400 grit) and run it lightly over the carving, with the grain; include the very edge, which will be slightly worn over, but be careful not to lose the crisp lines of the carving. Do not use wire wool on naked mahogany – I find it can react like oak and leave a blue sheen.

Take a stiff brush and vigorously remove the dust; this process should also burnish up the wood surface a little. This part of the post is now finished and ready for French polishing, for which the whole post is glued up first.

High relief

CHAPTER 9

PATERA

I n Chapters 7 and 8 I covered the basic principles and techniques of low relief carving. I defined its main quality as being 'flat' – in the sense of there being little depth with which to model. Hence, with the stool carving, you could literally put a ruler flat across its principal surfaces. The four-poster carving is also 'flat' in the sense of being very shallow, even though the carving is into a curved piece of wood.

If the background is reduced further, the carving becomes deeper, and the relief becomes 'higher'. At some fairly arbitrary point the work enters the realm of 'high relief' and eventually, if the ground were taken away completely, the subject may appear 'in the round'. As I said in Chapter 7, the boundary between low, medium and high relief is blurred, and often a piece will contain varying depths of relief carving. In higher relief carving there is much more three-dimensional movement of planes, the work loses its essential flatness and undercutting becomes more pronounced.

In this book you will see quite a few ways in which carving and turning combine to decorate certain parts of furniture. In this chapter I will look at another quite common piece of decoration – the patera (see Fig 9.1). While not the highest relief, it is an example of much higher relief carving than has been

INTRODUCTION

FIG 9.1 THE CARVED PATERA IN LIMEWOOD.

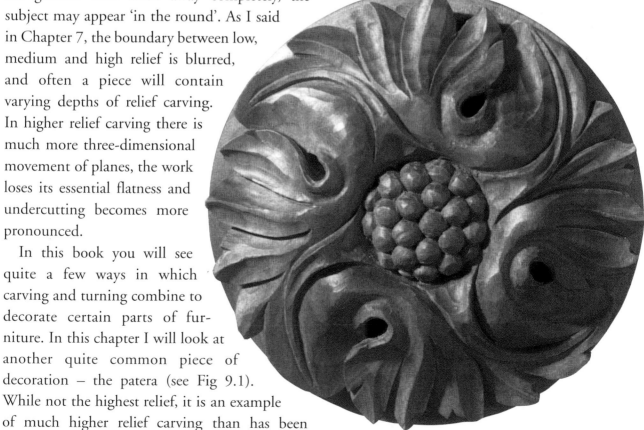

undertaken so far, and in it you can see the more three-dimensional qualities characteristic of higher relief developing.

'Patera' is a Latin word meaning a flat, circular ornament; the plural is technically 'paterae' but everyone I know says 'pateras'. Such ornaments are typically found on the ends of a frieze or decorating the tops of pilasters in fireplace surrounds. You may also see pateras on the square pommels of chair legs or bedposts. In such places the patera is normally 'applied' – made separately and fixed to the work later. A great deal of carving is 'applied' to other work in this sense, but as far as I know the patera is the only one that involves turning.

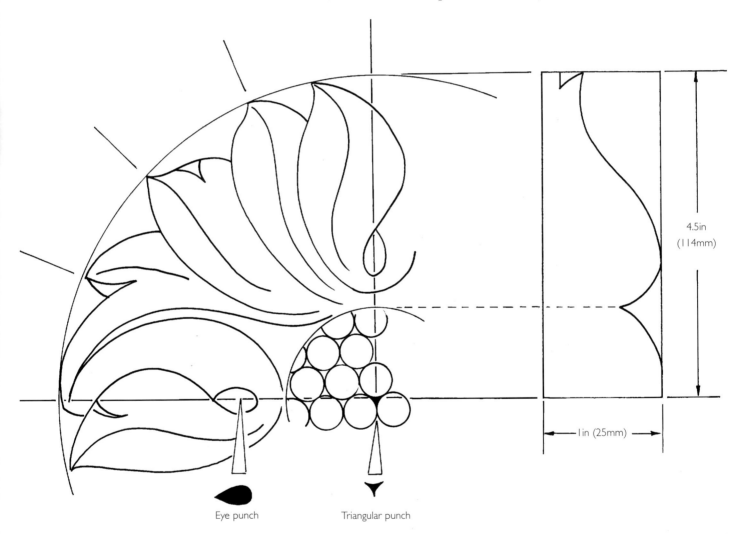

Eye punch   Triangular punch

4.5in (114mm)

1in (25mm)

FIG 9.2 WORKING DRAWING OF THE PATERA, SHOWING THE PROFILE, DIMENSIONS AND THE SHAPES OF THE TWO PUNCHES USED IN THIS PROJECT.

The plain turned patera is an item that many turners will be familiar with. One version involves turning a circular pattern with a centre boss or 'button' into a flat *square* of wood using a chuck screw. This square is then included in the corners of a fire surround, where the tops of the pilasters and ends of the horizontal frieze meet. Even if the frieze is left plain, the little bit of turning adds enormously to the finished work. The square itself, however, is not strictly a patera. If you were to turn the same design as a separate circular unit and then pin and glue it on to the blank square, *then* you have a patera.

This sort of basic turned patera lends itself very well to some of the simple carving effects I have already looked at in the previous chapters. The style of patera I made here is based on similar pateras found on furniture in the style of Louis XVI. Remember, should you decide to carve a pair of pateras, there is often the possibility of making them 'handed' – one winding to the left, the other to the right. I am only showing one patera being carved, but you might like to consider making two and handing them. Whatever design you choose, don't forget to work out a full-size drawing, and the exact cross-section before you begin work (see Fig 9.2).

Project: Patera

Turning

First, you must turn the patera profile, and then carve it. I used a piece of limewood about 4½in (114mm) in diameter and 1in (25mm) thick, although normally the wood is selected to match the piece of furniture to which the carving will be applied. Lime is a lovely wood to turn and carve, and also has a wonderful smell, which reminds me of frankincense. You can also consider the possibility of mixing woods. However, avoid using open-grained woods such as oak for this sort of work as they are poor at taking detail. Strongly figured woods are also inappropriate. A tight-grained pine is suitable providing you have sharp carving tools – which of course you have!

It is important that the turning creates the profile for the carving. You are in effect doing preliminary carving work on the lathe, and the finished appearance of the carving will depend on the profile you turn. As a result there is a great deal of scope for experimentation here.

FIG 9.3 SHAPING THE BASIC PATERA
WITH A SPINDLE GOUGE. THE
UNDERCUTTING OF THE EDGE, AND
CENTRE 'BUTTON', HAVE ALREADY
BEEN DONE USING THE SKEW CHISEL
AS A SCRAPER.

The circular blank is bandsawn a little oversize and an appropriate hole bored in the back to take a screw chuck. (I used a multichuck.) You can also screw the wood to a small faceplate, or use the paper and glue method to mount the blank on to a waste piece and then the faceplate. If you are making more than one patera then you need to be sure the profile is accurately repeated. Normal turning methods can be used here, but you might like to make a stiff template for finally checking. A little difference is permissible as the pateras are normally too far apart for close comparison, but you should aim for as close a match as possible and of course make no sacrifice of the quality of relief.

Mount the work on the lathe and true up the diameter. I found the best tools for shaping the profile quickly were a ½in (13mm)

FIG 9.4 A WOODCARVER'S SCREW
INSERTED INTO THE BACK OF THE
WORKPIECE.

skew chisel, used partly like a scraper and a ⅜in (10mm) spindle gouge (see Fig 9.3). Make the centre button round with the edges deep and sharp where the leaves will finally roll out from it. Do not undercut the leaves at the edge too much, or 'kick' them up excessively, as this will weaken them.

Get a smooth finish to the profile – there is no need to sand as the surface will be completely carved. To help drawing out the patera, divide the outer rim into eight and run a few strategically-placed circular lines.

Carving tools

The tools I used for this carving were more varied than those used for low relief work, due to the more extensive modelling required. You will need the ¼in (6mm) V tool and gouges to suit the sizes and shapes of the leaves. Make the cuts of the leaves with the edges of the gouges, creating crisp lines which should be full of flair.

Carving

Carve the patera at the bench. I found the simplest way to hold the patera is to insert a woodcarver's screw into the centre hole in the back of the patera which had previously been used to mount the piece for turning (see Fig 9.4). The shank of the screw passes through a board and the patera is tightened to it using the fly. The board itself is then held in an ordinary bench vice. The woodcarver's screw is a useful holding device to know about, but a fat wood screw would hold the patera to the board just as well. The advantage of the woodcarver's screw is that the fly is easily loosened to reposition the work.

Draw only the main lines of the carving, using the working drawing and divisions as your guide. As a principle in both carving and turning, you only need draw what is necessary for your next step – anything else will be immediately cut away and is therefore a waste of time.

You will see that there are four principal leaves, the edges of which radiate from junctions that make four 'eyes'. Set the eyes in first using a small semicircular gouge to start with (see Fig 9.5), followed by a flatter gouge to shape. The lobe that comes directly from the eye should also be set in early. Use a gouge that matches the curve you need and set in the edge of the leaf vertically, matching a second cut to the side to relieve the leaf (see Fig 9.6). You need to follow the

FIG 9.5 SETTING IN THE 'EYES'. NOTE THE SIMPLE DRAWING THAT GUIDES INITIAL CUTS.

FIG 9.6 SEPARATING THE MAIN LEAF THAT ARISES FROM THE EYE.

FIG 9.7 THE CENTRE VEIN IS
DELINEATED WITH THE V TOOL.

downward sweep of the turned profile, which adds a lot of the flair
to the carving.

Some undercutting of the edge of the lobe can be done as you
clean up – enough to create a clear shadow and sense of separation,
but not so much as to render the leaf weak. This is an important
point; remember that the patera may be subject to handling and
must therefore be reasonably robust.

Next, carve the main veins in between the eyes with a V tool (see
Fig 9.7). Tilt the V tool to the waste side; the background can be
cleared away with a subsequent stroke. Again, respect the turned
profile as you run the vein down to the point of the leaf in a flowing

FIG 9.8 SHAPING AROUND THE EYE
WITH A SMALL QUICK GOUGE.

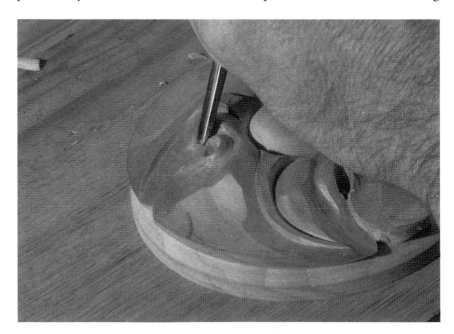

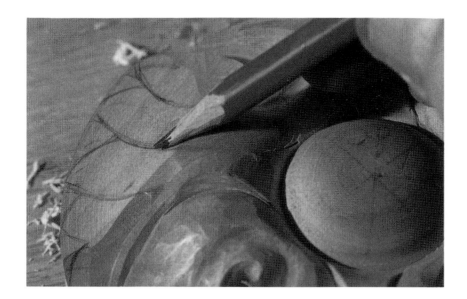

FIG 9.9 NEW DETAILS CAN NOW BE DRAWN IN — THE POSITION OF THE LEAF LOBES.

curve, becoming more shallow nearer the tip.

Model the area around the eyes and into the leaf lobes on either side. To accomplish this, use a small quick gouge 'upside down' over the top of the eye, and one similar to the eye tool down the sides (see Fig 9.8).

You will now have the rough form of the four principal leaves. The next step is to subdivide the leaves into their smaller lobes. Start by drawing them in, making sure they are fairly evenly placed (see Fig 9.9).

Use the V tool to separate the lobes of the leaves down into their lower edges (see Fig 9.10). Lean the tool over as before to undercut

FIG 9.10 SEPARATING THE LEAVES WITH THE V TOOL.

FIG 9.11 CLEANING UNDER THE
LEAVES — A SMALL, FLAT FISHTAIL
GOUGE IS IDEAL HERE.

FIG 9.11 CLEANING UNDER THE
LEAVES — A SMALL, FLAT FISHTAIL
GOUGE IS IDEAL HERE.

the leaves a little, and try to flow the lines. Use gouges with the appropriate sweep to set in the ends of the leaves and a skew chisel or fishtail gouge to clean out underneath (see Figs 9.11 and 9.12). You may need to angle the board holding the patera in a vice, perhaps holding it vertically in order to get at the underside or the leaves without developing a crick in your neck.

The patera should now be looking something like the finished version, so you can start modelling the leaves and making them more

FIG 9.12 SETTING IN EDGES OF THE
LEAVES WITH SELECTED GOUGES,
UNDERCUTTING INTO THE GROOVE
BENEATH.

interesting. Clean up the surface with small flat gouges, modelling the leaves and centre stem (see Fig 9.13). Take a side view of the patera to check that your lines are true and smooth. Nick the edges of a few leaves to suggest smaller lobes – it is this sort of detail which adds that extra touch.

Now for the centre button. The way to carve the little balls is very similar to the way the berries are carved in Chapter 10, only on a smaller scale. Take a semicircular gouge with whatever diameter of ball you require and set it vertically somewhere in the centre of the button. Rotate the edge against the wood and you will see it returns to the point it started from, cutting a neat circle. Just score the wood for now. Mark another circle next to it and so on until the button is entirely and neatly covered with circles. Going back to the first circle, deepen the cut and then use the gouge upside down to shape the ball. Be careful, as it is easy for the little ball to pop off, another good reason why a close-grain wood is preferable for this kind of carving. Work through all the balls in turn, always paying attention to the corners, which may need a little help from a skew chisel. As a finishing touch, take a triangular punch (which can be made by grinding or filing a thick nail) and tap it into the corners to clean and sharpen them (see Fig 9.14).

The eyes themselves also need punching (there must be a better way of saying that!) using the eye punch, which was used in Chapter

FIG 9.13 AFTER MODELLING THE CENTRE VEIN, MODELLING THE LEAVES CAN BEGIN.

FIG 9.14 BECAUSE THE SWEEP OF A
GOUGE IS PART OF A CIRCLE IT CAN BE
ROTATED TO MAKE THE SMALL BALLS.
THESE ARE THEN ROUNDED OVER
USING THE SAME GOUGE. A PUNCH
WITH A TRIANGULAR POINT WILL
CLEAN AND DEFINE THE JUNCTIONS
BETWEEN THE BALLS.

8 when carving the leaves of the vase. This will deepen the eyes and flatten their bottom surfaces, emphasizing them by producing more shadow. The shapes of both these punches are shown in Fig 9.2.

Finishing

Make a final check around the junction between leaves and centre button, looking for any tears or rough areas, and clean these up with the gouges. There is no need to sand.

And that's the patera. Posher than the ones that turners normally produce for fire surrounds I admit, but a good demonstration of high relief carving. You can see how much more depth there is in this type of carving, how undercutting can become a feature, and how the initial turning was used to create the deep, supporting profile, and you will hopefully be able to apply these techniques to other pieces in the future.

Furniture I

CHAPTER 10

GADROONS, PINEAPPLES AND BERRIES

Anyone who has made even the most superficial study of furniture will know that both turning and carving have long been employed as principal means of decorating otherwise plain pieces of work. Carving especially (as for example in Chippendale) has boldly gone where turning, with its axial volumes, has proved limited. Even so it is always surprising how just a small amount of appropriate and well worked turning or carving can enhance a table leg or some other element of furniture.

INTRODUCTION

Turners are often asked to make legs for tables and chairs. Sometimes the customer needs something more than just decorative turning, like a carved feature. By and large I have covered most of the techniques used in carving furniture already: the low relief of the milking stool (Chapter 7) and vase (Chapter 8) and the high relief of the patera (Chapter 9). Pierced relief is covered in Chapters 13 and 14. To take 'furniture carving' further the techniques described in these chapters must be supplemented with research. Take care to understand what is going on, draw a piece out accurately and relate it to the practices I have described. As there is no such thing as carving specifically for turners, there is also none specifically for furniture. Certainly there are specific patterns, but the techniques of woodcarving are transferable between all areas of interest. It is worth studying furniture as an aid to designing, even if you don't want to carve it as such, as it is a rich source of inspiration for turning and carving.

In this chapter I will look at a few common, fruity sounding decorative elements which a turner may be asked to produce in relation to furniture, starting with the 'gadroon' and moving on to 'pineapples' and 'berries'. In all of these a strong effect is produced by means of simple carving techniques.

I usually advise students to make a practice post – a bit of turning on which to work out and practise these designs – which can end up

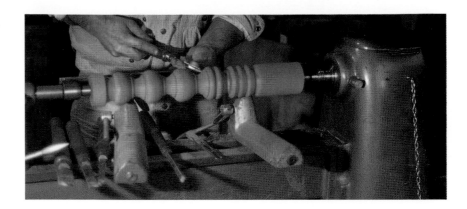

as a 'sampler' to keep to show customers their options (see Fig 10.1). The subjects are placed one above the other on a post. Make the post any size you want; the post shown is about 2½in (64mm) in diameter. Remember that increasing the diameter will have an effect on the appearance, and you may like to try different sizes.

So choose your size, round it to a cylinder and shape the practice profiles as follows:

- The sort of 'bulb' shape you need for a gadroon is shown in Fig 10.2.
- For the berries, you need to check that you have a semicircular carving gouge (number 9), and turn your bead to the width of this tool (see Fig 10.3).

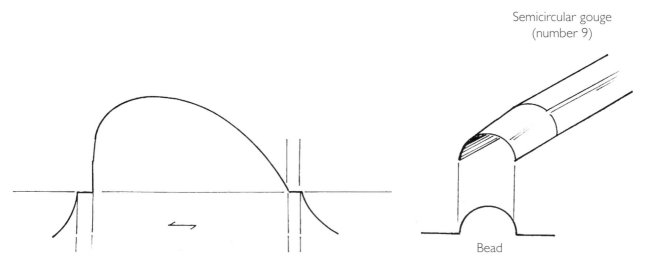

FIG 10.2 THE BASIC PROFILE OF A
GADROON, WITH THE UPPER PORTION
TO THE LEFT.

Semicircular gouge
(number 9)

Bead

FIG 10.3 THERE IS A DIRECT
RELATIONSHIP BETWEEN THE
GOUGE AND THE BERRIES IT WILL
CUT.

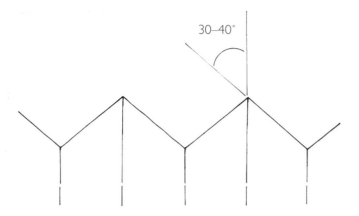

FIG 10.4 TURN THE RIDGES FOR THE PINEAPPLE AT A LOW ANGLE; TOO HIGH AND THEY BECOME TOO SHARP AND WEAK.

- For the pineapple, turn equal ridges no narrower than the width of your carving chisel – although for these a single-bevelled carpenter's chisel will also do the job (see Fig 10.4). Relate the distance between the ridges to the circumference, so that you end up with square pyramid shapes.

As always, make your turning crisp and even, especially the fillets which mark the changes in plane or direction in turned work (see Fig 10.5). I would suggest that you don't sand the parts to be carved, this

FIG 10.5 THE GADROONS AND OTHER PATTERNS CARVED IN THIS CHAPTER IN THE FORM OF A 'SAMPLER'.

will only serve to blunt your tools and there will be an opportunity to sand later.

You can carve the turning on the lathe, as I have done previously. This means you *must* be able to lock the wood in position – a lockable indexing plate is ideal. Alternatively you can remove the workpiece and hold it, as I do, in a vice on your workbench. The vice you can see in the photograph is the carver's 'chops' – the advantage of these lie in the jaws lifting the work above the bench. I gripped one end in the chops and let the other rest on the bench surface.

Project: Gadroons, pineapples and berries

GADROONS

'Gadroon' is one of my favourite words. I can imagine Shakespeare rolling it off his tongue, although it actually comes from 18th century French for 'a pleat or crease' and applies to the curved lines that divide up a bulb or rounded section of turning into lobes, so the bard missed out. He would have seen gadrooning though, under a different name. The effect first seems to have come to prominence in the Tudor–Stuart style of furniture as a way of lightening up the heavy, bulbous 'melon' style table legs. Although gadroon originally meant a crease, it now refers to the lobe effect. I will take 'gadroon' and 'lobe' to mean the same thing – furniture makers go even further and actually use the verb 'gadrooning'.

There are many styles of gadroons, some more complicated than others. Some table legs of this period are over three times the diameter of our practice post. There can be fewer, or more, divisions. The sweep of the gadroon profile also makes a difference to the final appearance, especially on the larger sizes of leg where the top of the gadroon finishes almost at right angles with the axis.

I carved a basic style with a couple of variations. I divided the turned 'bulb' into 16 parts, marking the lines to cut as accurately as I could, axially, on the wood. You can experiment with fewer lines, making wider gadroons.

Carving tools

The carving tools I used in this project were:

V tool x ¼in (6mm).
Skew or small fishtail chisel.
No. 5 x ¼in (6mm).
No. 9 x ¼in (6mm) (basically a small quick gouge).

I used the number 5 for the sides, tops and bottoms of the gadroon. You may find that, if your profile is different, especially diameters at top and bottom, or if you want something more rounded, you will need a different size gouge.

Carving

Starting with the simplest form, the first step is to separate the individual gadroons with the V tool. Note that you need to work in opposite directions from the maximum circumference of the gadroon, cutting downhill *with the grain* (see Fig 10.6). On the lathe this means swapping over hands or reversing the work; on the bench the piece is simply turned around. Complete half of the grooving before you turn it back again or you'll be forever swapping back and forth. Do not run the V tool into the fillets at either end. Try to flow the tool round to follow the curve and run along the centre line (see Fig 10.7).

FIG 10.6 RUNNING THE GROOVES THAT SEPARATE THE GADROONS.

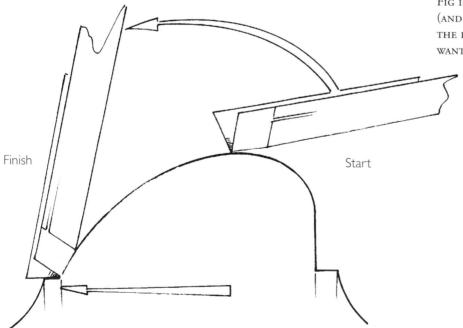

Finish

Start

FIG 10.7 TRY TO RUN THE V TOOL (AND THE GOUGE) SMOOTHLY ALONG THE PROFILE OF THE SHAPE YOU WANT.

FIG 10.8 ROUNDING OVER THE EDGES
OF EACH GADROON WITH AN
INVERTED GOUGE.

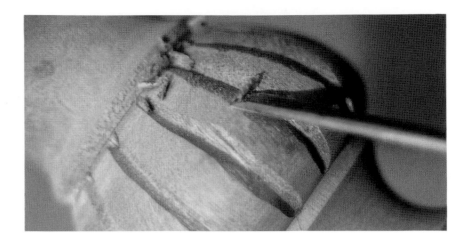

When the divisions have been made, take a gouge with a profile that approximates to the gadroon, turn it 'upside down' so that the mouth is against the wood and round over each corner of the gadroon into its characteristic lobe-like shape, trying to merge the cuts in the middle (see Fig 10.8). You will find that you will need a different sweep of gouge for the fatter ends of the gadroon to that needed for the narrower end. Turn the workpiece round as before to work *with* the grain.

Flow with the curve as you did with the V tool and try not to leave 'flats'. You may need to firm up the centre groove with the V tool again. As before don't run the gouge into the fillet, but stop exactly short.

You will have to shape the ends of the gadroon with the gouge – this is where your selection of gouge is important. If you can set in with one cut you will have a perfect end (see Fig 10.9).

Clean between the ends of the gadroon with a small fishtail or skew chisel. You may find that the fillet is not now parallel with the

FIG 10.9 REMOVING THE WOOD
BETWEEN GADROONS. USE THE
BOTTOM OF THE DIVISION BETWEEN
LOBES AS A GUIDE TO THE SHAPE.

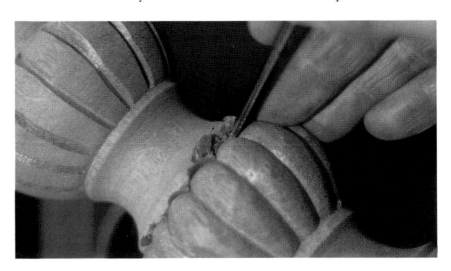

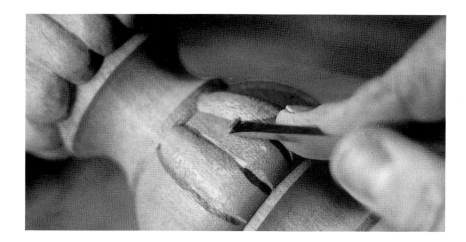

FIG 10.10 SHAPING THE LOWER ENDS
NEATLY UP TO THE FILLET. THE TOP
ENDS ARE FINISHED IN A SIMILAR
FASHION. THE SAME GOUGE CAN BE
USED, OR DIFFERENT ONES,
DEPENDING ON THE CURVATURE
REQUIRED.

axis but slopes inwards a little. This is perfectly acceptable as long as you are consistent with all the table legs you are carving.

You should now have the basic gadroon shape with a series of lobes. Depending on the work, you can finish the surfaces nicely with the carving tools or sand them finely. Some variation is natural to hand work but do try and make the lines *appear* true. You have now carved the humblest form of the gadroon.

Gadroon and scoop

For this variation on the basic pattern you need an even number of divisions. Carve every other gadroon as before, but flatten the intermediate ones by cutting away the wood with a small chisel (see Fig 10.10). Follow the curve made by the base of the gadroon and keep the junction neat. Set in the lower end of the gadroons as the normal shape.

Now use a fairly quick gouge to 'scoop' a trough into the flat sections (see Fig 10.11). The 'top end' of the scoop runs up against

FIG 10.11 SCOOPING OUT A TROUGH
WITH A 'QUICK' GOUGE.

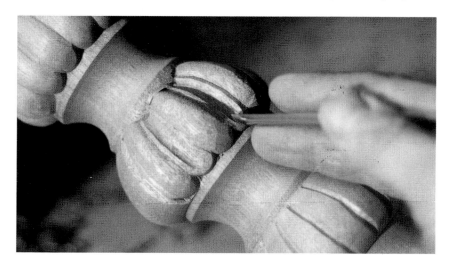

FIG 10.12 RELIEVING THE SIDES WITH
THE GOUGE TO CREATE THE DART.

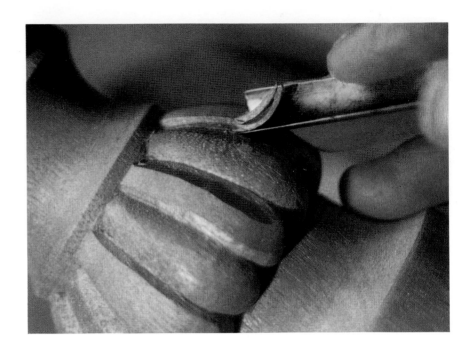

the fillet and is finished off with the fishtail or skew chisel. Again the piece can be finished neatly or sanded smooth.

Gadroon and dart

This is a second variation on the original gadroon. Carve every other lobe or gadroon as for the first version, so that in between each gadroon will be the original turning, untouched. Set in the lower ends of each division as before. Use a gouge in the usual way (mouth uppermost) to cut a cove down the edge of these untouched sections to produce a ridge along the centre; this is the dart (see Fig 10.12). You may like to draw a centre line to help you. A variation on this is to make more of an arrow head to each dart (see Fig 10.13).

There are several more things you can do to make the humble gadroon more sophisticated, including carving leaves in between lobes, which you will find illustrated in furniture books.

FIG 10.13 TWO MORE VARIATIONS TO
THE GADROON: A CHIP-CARVED FILLET
(LEFT) AND A DART-END (RIGHT).

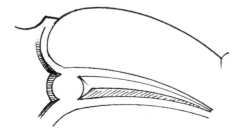
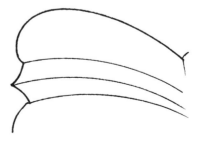

Most often seen on Victorian four-posters, the pineapple looks best in a spiral form, when it does indeed resemble those strange fruits (see Fig 10.14). The effect is also seen on finials where the little lozenges diminish in size towards the top. For this project I made parallel cuts, without any spiral effect, to a cylindrical part which was turned as part of the practice post. Each square or lozenge is a little four-sided pyramid.

Mark the squares out accurately. On the post you should have turned an accurate series of ridges. Now divide the circumference up so that you outline each *square* of the pineapple. Divide again to find the centre point of the pyramids-to-be. It is absolutely essential that you mark out carefully and accurately to achieve a good result.

Carving tools

The only tool you need is a chisel, preferably a size that is the length of one side of the squares.

Carving

Start with a vertical stop cut on the line between the ridges. Follow this with two angled cuts which start at the point of the ridge and meet neatly in the centre, removing a chip of wood (see Fig 10.15). Keep repeating this pattern of cuts, finishing each V-shaped cut nicely before moving on and you will see the pineapple effect form before your eyes (see Fig 10.16). Even though working on a large pineapple can be rather tedious, work methodically and pay attention to getting each cut clean.

PINEAPPLES

FIG 10.14 A TRUE 'PINEAPPLE' SPIRALLING ROUND THE TURNING TO PRODUCE LOZENGE-SHAPED PYRAMIDS.

FIG 10.15 THE TURNED RIDGES ARE FIRST MARKED OUT. THE LINES ARE, ALTERNATELY, POINTS AND INTERSECTIONS OF PYRAMIDS. AN INITIAL STOP CUT CONTROLS SUBSEQUENT WOOD REMOVAL. THEN THE SIDES OF THE PYRAMIDS ARE INDIVIDUALLY CUT.

FIG 10.16 FINISHED SAMPLE OF
PINEAPPLE CARVING.

You can work with or across the grain. Be careful when working *with* the grain as you are actually working *parallel* to it and you may find the grain splits away in front of the cutting edge. I always work across the grain, slicing my cut wherever possible.

A true pineapple has its lozenges spiralling around. To achieve this you need to follow the setting out that is described for the barley twists in Chapter 11. Instead of turning the ridges, use the same saw technique, cleaned up with a V tool, and cut the first set of spiral ridges with a chisel. You are carving the ridge effect which you initially produced in the previous example on the lathe, only here you are carving *spiral* ridges, not the circumferential ridges, which are all the lathe is capable of. Then chip out the remaining sides of the lozenges as above. A tapered finial uses a similar technique.

BERRIES

Berries, and variations on the design such as 'sausages and berries', go back into classical times as runs of mouldings around borders. A moulding, in carving, is a repeated pattern which forms a border or edge to a panel, acting like a frame. The berry moulding is often used with leaf-like mouldings in this context. For the turner, however, it can comfortably be used on its own to contrast other shapes and details.

Carving tools

The secret of carving berries properly is to look to your gouge first.

You must pick a gouge with a sweep (or inside curvature) which is the same as the starting bead you are turning. Carvers place rows of berries in all sorts of strange places. To do this they cut the initial bead (from which the berries are carved) with the same gouge with which they will subsequently carve them, inverting the gouge and running an exact bead. However, the only beads available to the turner are those worked around the diameter of a cylinder, so it is important that you do not make the bead larger or smaller than the semicircular gouge you intend to use.

Carving

The intersection of each berry can be marked either with dividers, or simply by marking the wood using the corners of the gouge you intend to use.

The knack in carving the berries is to wind the gouge over, starting at a tangent to the top of the berry to finish upright at its base — in a similar way to which I carved the gadroons. This is done on one side of the berry and then on the opposite side; you can even rotate the blade around the berry (see Fig 10.17). You may like to make a few tentative preliminary cuts to start with. If you have a lot of difficulty — and after all you have to not only get the berry a good shape but run the line of berries around a cylinder — I suggest you use a flat piece of wood for some preliminary practice.

Make the semicircular bead with a V tool and the inverted gouge,

Fig 10.18 The gouge can be turned at right angles to shape the berry down to the fillets. The wedges between the berries are cleaned up with a small fishtail chisel.

and you should end up with small triangular waste pieces. Nick these out with a small fishtail or skew chisel (see Fig 10.18). Most beginners end up with a flattish top and steep sides. It is almost axiomatic in carving that you must really *visualize the form* for which you are aiming and follow the imaginary shape with the cutting edge. Try your best to get a nice fat rounded form to these berries.

There are several other variations of this simple technique, and it is the sort of thing that looks very good on the lids of boxes.

Only a few carving tools are required to produce the three designs – gadroons, pineapples and berries – which have featured in this chapter. Accurate marking out and clean cutting will produce quite strong and effective decorations, whose impact on the whole piece of work can be considerable.

Furniture II

CHAPTER 11

BARLEY TWISTS

'Barley twists' may fool the unwary – who think them tasty
confection-ary, but lick one from the turner's shop, and you'll
find that splinters make you stop.

At the risk of gaining, or losing, a reputation as a poet, I include this bit of doggerel to show the state of mind one gets into when carving too many barley twists. While not difficult, they require an awful lot of dedicated patience to get them just right, and especially to achieve that fine surface finish which catches the light so attractively when polished up. So, be warned, too many and one's mind starts to wander!

INTRODUCTION

FIG 11.1 BAROQUE BARLEY TWISTS ON THE ALTAR OF A CHURCH IN BAVARIA.

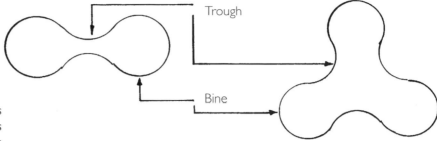

FIG II.2 BINES AND TROUGHS ALWAYS OCCUR IN EQUAL NUMBERS — IN THIS CASE, DOUBLE AND SINGLE BINE BARLEY TWISTS.

The barley twist gets its name from a Victorian confectionery but in fact, as a decorative element, the design goes back much further. In this country, they made their first appearance on furniture in the middle of the seventeenth century, shortly after the civil war. Some magnificent examples of sculptured columns are to be found in the Rococo churches of southern Germany, and Fig 11.1 shows what you can do with barley twists if you have the ambition!

Let me begin with some terms. The **bine** is the prominent ridge that winds around the barley twist, and the **trough** is the hollow recess between two bines (see Fig 11.2). All barley twists must have the same number of bines as troughs. If there is one bine (and one trough) the form is called a **single bine**, which is the subject of the first carving in this chapter. If there are two bines (and two troughs), the form is called a double bine (see Fig 11.3), and so on. The higher the number, the tighter the feel. On narrow spindles, a few bines work well, and larger numbers work better on thicker stock, as in four-poster bedposts.

If the bines are made prominent, and the troughs reduced to grooves, you have the **rope twist**, often used in chair backs (see Fig 11.4). If the trough is given prominence and the bine reduced to a crest you have, for want of a better term, a **hollow twist** – which is

FIG II.3 DOUBLE BINE BARLEY TWIST STAIR SPINDLE, IN OAK.

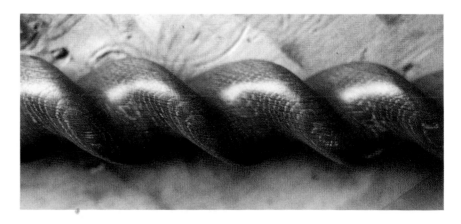

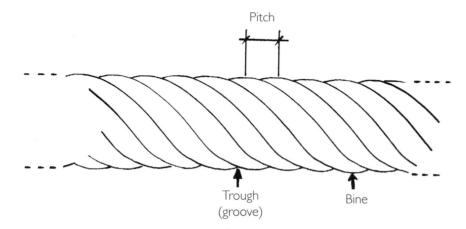

Pitch

Trough
(groove)

Bine

FIG II.4 A 'ROPE' TWIST.

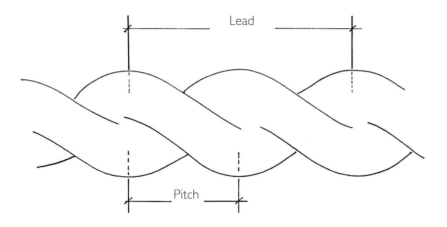

Lead

Pitch

FIG II.5 'LEAD' AND 'PITCH' IN A
DOUBLE BINE BARLEY TWIST.

the subject of the second carving in this chapter.

The **pitch** is the distance between bines along the same longitudinal line (see Fig 11.5), and depends largely on the number of bines you want – which will be your first decision. The rope twist has the smallest possible pitch, and the single bine the largest. Each number option gives a different appearance.

The **lead** is the distance along the cylinder that a bine takes to make one complete revolution (see Fig 11.5). As a guide, a lead of about twice the diameter of the original cylinder is commonly used, which gives a 'tilt' of about 45° to the twist; a comfortable angle. The choice of angle must be your second decision.

As I have said, the two barley twist types that feature in this chapter are the single bine and the hollow twist. Both were replacements for broken parts – twists are not strong structures, and this sort of replacement work crops up regularly for trade turners. These two examples should cover all the basic techniques you need to deal with any other style of barley twist.

Project: Barley twists

Turning

In each case the spindle was first turned in the normal 'between centres' fashion, with an accurate cylindrical section for the carving. Note the groove at each end of the cylinder; this allows the barley twist to finish nicely and in a logical manner (refer to Fig 11.8). Barley twists are normally cylindrical in pattern, but *may* taper.

There is no need to sand the cylinder for the initial carving stages – a clean surface from the roughing gouge is quite adequate.

You will also need to make a supporting saddle that tucks underneath the spindle while you are carving it, as once the wood becomes thinner, it can flex alarmingly. You will see a trough-like saddle that fits in the toolrest holding post in use throughout the carving (refer to Fig 2.13).

Marking out

Isolate the lathe once the turning is finished, as from now on it will

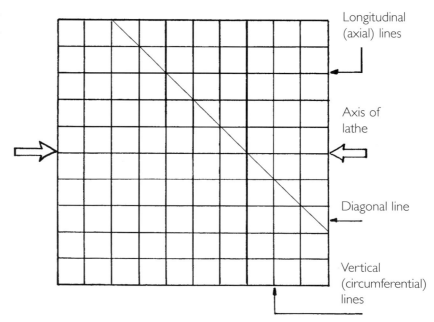

FIG 11.6 USE GRAPH PAPER TO REPRESENT THE LINES YOU WILL DRAW ON THE CYLINDER.

Longitudinal (axial) lines

Axis of lathe

Diagonal line

Vertical (circumferential) lines

act only to support the carving.

Having decided the number of bines and troughs, and the lead, you need to draw centre lines that follow the paths of the bines and troughs around the cylinder. Do this with the wood still on the lathe.

A one-off twist can be marked well enough by wrapping masking tape around the spindle. The problem comes when you need to repeat the pattern accurately, or carve left- and right-handed twists, and for this you need to mark accurately:

- Longitudinal divisions – relating to the number of bines and troughs.
- A series of lines around the cylinder – for the pitch.

One way to study how these twists 'work' is by drawing lines on a piece of graph paper and rolling it up (see Figs 11.6 and 11.7). Some people find this helps them visualize more clearly what is going on.

Mark these longitudinal and circumferential divisions so that the lines of troughs and bines can be easily drawn. This will become a little more obvious in the worked examples.

If there are four bines, mark eight, equally-spaced, longitudinal lines – including four for the troughs – using the lathe toolrest to guide the pencil. An indexing plate is extremely helpful here. For three bines divide lengthwise into six, and so on.

FIG 11.7 ROLLING UP THE GRAPH PAPER ILLUSTRATES HOW THE LINES DIRECT THE BINES AND TWISTS.

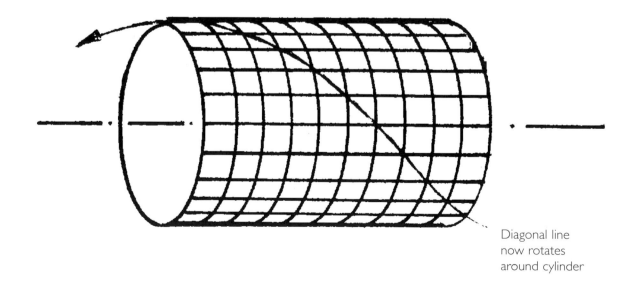

Diagonal line now rotates around cylinder

Carving and shaping tools

Barley twists are more of a shaping than a carving exercise, and of course the tool size will vary with work size. The tools I was using in this project were:

Tenon saw.
A large V tool (an alternative to the tenon saw for the second twist).
Chisel x 1–1½in (25–38mm).
Carving gouge, deep curve x ½in (13mm).
Carving gouge, shallow curve x ½in (13mm).
Rasps and files.
Sandpaper.

In both the carvings, the spindle is locked firmly by the indexing plate. If you don't have one, then you must find some other way of locking the mandrel to prevent the work rotating or slipping beneath the effort.

Carving

Let's start with the single bine. Fig 11.8 shows the original broken barley twist, in rosewood, and the basic cylinder copy below it.

There is one bine and one trough. I needed to mark a rotating line for each – two lines, and therefore two starting points. To make the drawing of the rotating lines easier, I added extra longitudinal lines in between. The cylinder is thus divided into four longitudinal lines.

To get the correct pitch – where the bine will reappear further along – cylindrical lines were drawn on, spinning the spindle between centres. The position was taken from the original barley twist pattern

FIG 11.8 THE ORIGINAL ABOVE, AND THE STARTING CYLINDER BELOW, UNSANDED EXCEPT FOR THE END BEADS, AND MARKED OUT. NOTE THE GROOVE AT EACH END OF THE CYLINDER. THE CONTINUOUS LINE OF THE BINE IS IN RED, THE TROUGH IN BLACK. THE PITCH OF THE SINGLE LINE IS SHOWN BY THE DOTS.

FIG 11.9 SAWING TO DEPTH COMPLETED WITH THE TENON SAW AND DEPTH GAUGE, RIGHT TO THE ENDS.

and divided as before to make subsequent drawing easier.

I now had a cylindrical graph, so to speak – as in the rolled up paper exercise above. I marked in the rotating lines of bine and trough by joining up the corners of the squares. I used different colours for each – not so important here, but when you have a large number of lines, it avoids confusion! In Fig 11.8 the pitch is shown by the distance between the red dots. If you are doing repeat work, remember to start the lines from the same point on the spindle each time; for example, related to a corner of any remaining square block.

I used a tenon saw, with a depth fence, to cut a groove that follows the trough line and cut down to just above the finishing depth (see Fig 11.9). Masking tape on the saw will do as a depth gauge. Keep within the waste wood and don't go too deep or you will have difficulty cleaning up the trough surface (see Fig 11.10). I had to make a series of cuts to work my way round.

Next take the chisel and cut away wood from the side of the bine, down into the trough, using the drawn bine line as a guide and

FIG 11.10 THE SAW CUT MUST KEEP WITHIN THE WASTE WOOD.

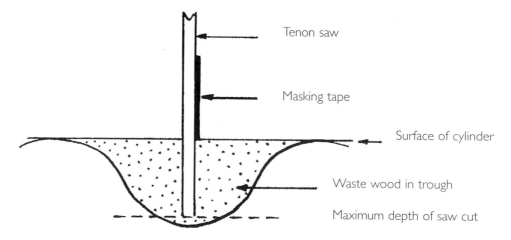

Tenon saw

Masking tape

Surface of cylinder

Waste wood in trough

Maximum depth of saw cut

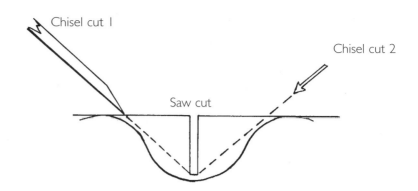

FIG 11.11 CHISEL AWAY THE WASTE WOOD TO THE BOTTOM OF THE SAW CUT.

Chisel cut 1

Chisel cut 2

Saw cut

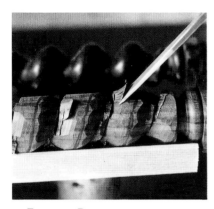

FIG 11.12 REMOVING THE WOOD IN THE TROUGH USING THE CHISEL, GOING WITH THE GRAIN.

FIG 11.13 KEEP A SENSE OF THE FORM BENEATH WHILE REVERSING THE GOUGE TO CLEAN UP THE BINE. NOTE THE BINE LINE STILL PRESENT.

going with the grain (see Figs 11.11 and 11.12). This line remains to the very end, being on the outermost surface. Remember the great carving principle: always work from the mass into the space – in this way you avoid taking away wood that you should be leaving. As always, try and get a sense of the form beneath as you work. Then reverse the spindle on the lathe to work the opposite side.

I used the gouge to remove waste from the trough. This is quicker than a rasp, but something like a Surform would do the job as well. I also used another gouge upside down to refine the shape of the bines (see Fig 11.13) but this can be done with the chisel if you haven't got the right gouge.

Once you've gone as far as you can with the carving tools, it's on to the rasps, files and sandpaper to clean up (see Fig 11.14); this is where it can get a little tedious and the poetry creeps in!

I find cloth-backed paper the best for rounding over the curves (see Fig 11.15). Try to sweep the rasps and sandpaper along the bines and troughs with a sense of the smooth form beneath, working through finer grits. Like a bowl, the grain in the barley twist goes in every direction, so care must be taken with the finish so as not to show scratch marks – especially if the work is to be French polished.

I kept referring to the original pattern to make sure it 'felt' the same. Remember to check the ends of the barley twist, as they always seem to get a bit neglected.

Moving on to the hollow twist, the emphasis here is on the bine, which is attenuated to a crest. Some very fine examples of this type of twist were used in Regency staircases. A good pattern book is *Mouldings and Turned Woodwork of the 16th, 17th and 18th Centuries*, details of which can be found in the bibliography.

The initial setting out is similar to the single bine. In this case however, four bines are marked, and the troughs could be marked in

FIG 11.14

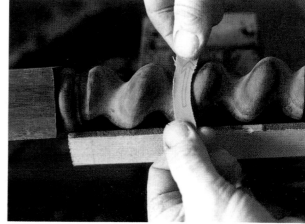

FIG 11.15

the spaces in between. As the crest of the bine is important and the trough not necessarily very deep, I often don't mark the centre of the trough but go straight in with a V tool (see Fig 11.16). I lined the tool up by eye and worked to just above the approximate depth.

It is worth noting at this point that if you are carving rope twists, you must chase this V cut around a trough line which has been drawn smoothly and accurately. Cut to depth and simply round over the bine into the groove.

When the V groove (which is in fact a stop cut) is finished on the hollow bine, start to remove the wood from one side, *with the grain*, using a suitable straight gouge (see Fig 11.17). Reverse the spindle on the lathe and work the other side down to, and merging with, the V groove.

FIG 11.14 A ROUND FILE CLEANS UP THE TROUGH.

FIG 11.15 CLOTH-BACKED SANDPAPER IS BEST FOR THE CURVED EDGES, WHILE PAPER AROUND SHAPED BLOCKS WILL REFINE THE HOLLOW SURFACES.

FIG 11.16 CUTTING A STOP GROOVE IN A HOLLOW TWIST WITH THE V TOOL.

FIG 11.17 WHEN ALL THE GROOVES ARE COMPLETE START REMOVING WOOD, WITH THE GRAIN, USING A STRAIGHT GOUGE.

FIG 11.16

FIG 11.17

FIG 11.18 CLEANING UP PRIOR
TO LIGHT RASPING.

Finishing

Go over the surface and clean it up (see Fig 11.18) before moving on to the rasps. As before, sweep the rasps around the twist sympathetically to get a true form, using your fingers to guide you. It's then on to sanding for a finish (see Fig 11.19).

There are many varieties of barley twist carving, and as turners tend to develop a clear eye for a line, this type of work should come relatively naturally. With accurate drawing out, you should have no trouble with the shaping, or indeed writing poetry!

One important, final point. It doesn't matter if the pitch is a little out, or the depth a little irregular, what matters is the *feeling*: the beauty of barley twists lies in the perfection of their curves, which has a great bearing on the way in which they rhythmically reflect the light.

FIG 11.19 RASP A GOOD SHAPE INTO
THE TROUGHS AND UP TO THE CRESTS
(NOTE THAT THE BINE LINE REMAINS
UNTIL THE END); THEN SAND WITH
CURVED BLOCKS TO A FINE FINISH.

Working in the round

CHAPTER 12

FROG BOX

The conventional way to teach carving begins with cutting various types of decorative patterns. A student would then move on to the lowest relief carving, then higher and higher relief, and only then would he or she start on truly three-dimensional work. This approach advances the student gradually, from simple to more difficult processes, and is one I generally find helpful and have been following so far in this book. Therefore, it is now time to attempt a bit of three-dimensional work.

INTRODUCTION

FIG 12.1 THE FINISHED FROG BOX.

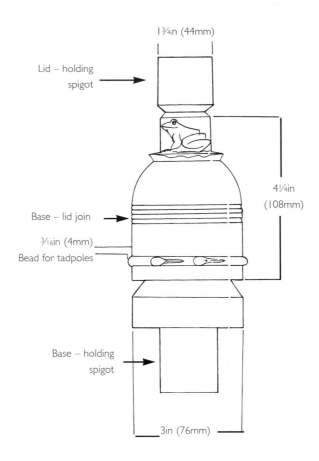

FIG 12.2 DETAILS AND DIMENSIONS
OF THE FROG BOX IN THE PROJECT.

1¾in (44mm)

Lid – holding
spigot

4¼in
(108mm)

Base – lid join

³⁄₁₆in (4mm)
Bead for tadpoles

Base – holding
spigot

3in (76mm)

I take the view that turners normally develop a better than average sense of three-dimensional form, but all their training is in axial volumes. In carving, the constraints of the lathe are broken, and there are far fewer limits to the direction a design can take. This freedom can be both liberating and intimidating at the same time to anyone starting to carve. Even turners, with their grasp of form and practical ability, usually share a sense of trepidation with every other beginner.

The cure lies in the correct approach to carving in the round, and a methodical way of working. In the frog box project look for the following important points:

- The importance of preliminary research and design.
- How work starts from 'high spots' – points on the surface from which wood is not removed.
- How carving proceeds from the masses into the spaces.
- The need to set in the main forms first, then refine them, and *only then* put in the details.

As with the other projects in this book, whether or not you attempt the project itself, it is important to gain an understanding of the techniques and approaches employed, so that you can apply these to your own designs.

The frog box (see Fig 12.1) was specifically requested by a ranophile, and my first thought on the design was to just carve a frog, the head of which came off to reveal the box. But this idea seemed either too surreal or too kitsch, I couldn't decide which, so a box with a frog *on* it, it had to be (see Fig 12.2).

The frog is the focal point, but it also acts as the handle to the box lid. Hence it had to be strong enough to take an amount of handling, for example by linking the frog's front elbows to its strong knees. It must have no uncomfortable corners and be firmly part of the lid. While it may seem 'more natural' for the frog to have landed by accident on the box, this would have made the carving a bit too advanced, though a better design.

I then needed something to balance the frog perched on the lid. I decided on a simple pattern of tadpoles swimming around the base. This *implies* depth by suggesting water beneath the leaf, and like the box itself, water is something into which objects are dropped. A further balance above and below came from echoing some added colour. Green was the most obvious, but have you seen those Central American Harlequin frogs?

I used a tight-grained tulip wood which takes green stain well and has an interesting variation in colour, creating a different appearance to each side of the box. I also love the smell of this wood.

For the appearance of the frog, I tried to strike a balance between realism and character (as opposed to caricature), and to some extent character won. I found illustrated children's books a great help as research material, and this applies to any kind of wildlife carving you may wish to attempt.

It is very important that you have in your mind a good idea of the frog's anatomy from three directions: above, the front, and the side (see Fig 12.3). This applies to any other carving in the round. If you are unsure, you should do a little more research – you don't want to remove wood you may need later – and it may help to make a model in clay or plasticine first.

DESIGN

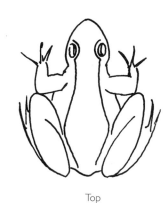

Top

Front

Side

FIG 12.3 BEFORE CARVING ANYTHING, YOU NEED TO HAVE A CLEAR IMPRESSION OF WHAT YOU WANT TO ACHIEVE. SIMPLE RESEARCH SKETCHES SUCH AS THESE ARE A GOOD START.

Project: Frog box

Turning

First of all, decide how the box will be held for carving. I decided that the end spigots arising from the initial turning would also provide the simplest means of holding it. The waste can be removed last of all.

I turned the box itself in the normal fashion, starting between centres and leaving waste spigots at *both* ends (see Fig 12.4). These are held in a chuck for hollowing out later. When you turn the block where the frog and leaf will be, try to be as helpful to the carved profile as possible, but if in doubt leave more, rather than less, material. Don't forget the bead that stands proud for the tadpoles.

Part the lid off as tightly as possible, so maintaining the grain. Then, gripping the spigot in a three-jaw chuck, form the lip that takes the lid. Finally, hollow out the base part of the box itself. Make the lid a good fit to the base *before* hollowing it and allow the top underneath the frog to be a little thicker and stronger (see Fig 12.5).

Note that the small beads that circle the lid-to-base join, eventually stained green, camouflage the join and add more interest to the centre part of the design. Finish the insides well and thin enough – there will be no need to return to them later.

Carving tools

The carving is small scale so I used very few tools, none wider than ¼in (6mm). Something like:

> Nos 2 (skew), 3 and 6 x ¼in (6mm).
> Nos 3, 6, 9 and V tool x ⅛in (3mm)
> No. 3 x 1⁄16in (2mm).

You may need a larger variety of tools to do the work than you have in your kit; it is here that you may have to think about enlarging your collection, based on what was said in Chapter 3 on tools and equipment.

Carving

Secure the lid to the base with masking tape – the carving is light

FIG 12.4

FIG 12.5

work without much stress on the lid. The base spigot is then held in a simple bench vice. Mine was a portable vice that clamped to the edge of the bench and, lined with cork, the jaws gripped the cylindrical spigot securely enough. I also held the box horizontally, and higher off the bench, in a more upright vice called carver's 'chops', but you will probably think of other options yourself. Whatever method you use, make sure you can adjust the work as you carve round it.

For the frog itself, first remove the waste spigot from the lid with a light saw, cleaning up with a flat gouge or chisel. Decide which direction, related to the figuring of the wood, you want the frog to face and draw a central line. Replace this line continually as the wood is carved away. It is a guide to symmetry only; the frog will look more real if it is a little asymmetrical.

You can work most of the time with and across the grain; you shouldn't need to work against the grain. If you can use the carving tools ambidextrously, so much the better. Remember to strop regularly.

My approach – and it is not that of every carver – was first to

FIG 12.4 TURNING THE OUTSIDE SHAPE OF THE BOX BETWEEN CENTRES.

FIG 12.5 THE LID BEING HOLLOWED, HELD BY THE SPIGOT. THE LID AND BASE MUST FIT WELL, AS THIS IS, AFTER ALL, A FUNCTIONAL BOX.

FIG 12.6

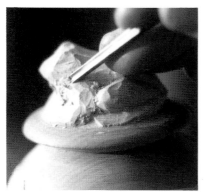

FIG 12.7

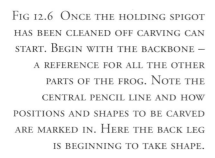

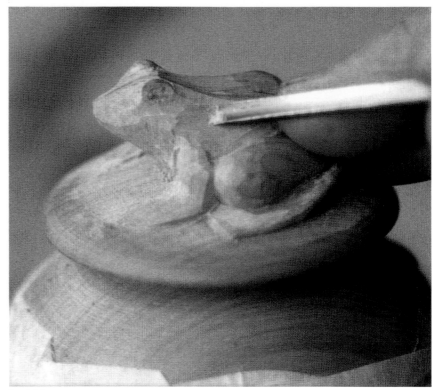

FIG 12.8

FIG 12.6 ONCE THE HOLDING SPIGOT HAS BEEN CLEANED OFF CARVING CAN START. BEGIN WITH THE BACKBONE – A REFERENCE FOR ALL THE OTHER PARTS OF THE FROG. NOTE THE CENTRAL PENCIL LINE AND HOW POSITIONS AND SHAPES TO BE CARVED ARE MARKED IN. HERE THE BACK LEG IS BEGINNING TO TAKE SHAPE.

FIG 12.7 MOVING TOWARDS THE SHOULDER AND FRONT LEG. NOTE HOW MY FINGER RESTS ON THE WOOD AND CONTROLS THE MOVEMENT OF THE TOOL. BY THIS STAGE, THE FRONT LEGS ARE APPEARING AND ARE BEGINNING TO SEPARATE FROM THE BODY.

FIG 12.8 CLEANING UP ALONG THE SIDE AS MODELLING STARTS.

mark positions on the starting block of *any surface points that will be present in the finished carving*. In this case the nose, tail and knees were marked.

I then carved the profile of the frog's backbone, marking further points such as the hip bones. Having established some fairly fixed points, I used these as references, working away from them, three-dimensionally, into the rest of the carving. I established other 'fixed points' wherever and whenever I could, using one reference point to establish another (see Fig 12.6). *Do not* put in detail at this stage, but try and establish the relative positions of the limbs and major parts.

From the back legs and knees I worked along the sides of the body towards the ankles and feet. I carved the two ridges along the frog's back up from the hip bones towards the eyes and, shaping these, I moved to the sides of the head and shoulder (see Fig 12.7). The carving then went down the shoulder to the front legs and under the head to the belly. One very important tip here: *work from the form into the hollows*, allowing holes to develop naturally. If you concentrate on the holes, these tend to get bigger and bigger! Always reposition the workpiece whenever you need to get to an area more easily.

When this stage is completed you should have a readily recognizable frog, having brought out the larger shapes and rhythms (see Fig 12.8). The next stage is to get some depth of cut and start modelling the details, marrying the frog to the leaf convincingly. This will mean a certain amount of undercutting, deepening clefts and adjusting relative positions. You want to remove the obvious circular quality of the turning, both from the frog and the leaf, yet leave the impression of their relationship with the cylinder. I hope you can see a parallel between what is occurring here and how a piece of pure turning is normally approached: first the principal and underlying masses and movements, *then* the details.

Outline and set in the feet as you model the leaf (see Fig 12.9). Do not undercut the leaf too much as the grain here is short and weak. You should be able to finish the frog without resorting to sandpaper, using sharp flat gouges for a final, clean surface, as you work with or across the grain.

Moving on to the tadpoles: mark these out first – all the same or different as you prefer – and reposition the box to get at them easily. We are now back to simple low relief carving. The background to the tadpoles is the surface of the box and its roundness must be

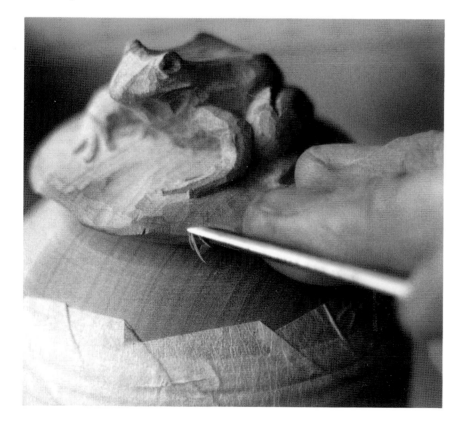

FIG 12.9 THE BELLY AND FRONT FEET HAVE BEEN DEFINED AND THE FROG LEAF JUNCTION CLEANED UP. HERE THE LEAF IS BEING SHAPED WITH A LIGHT AMOUNT OF UNDERCUTTING.

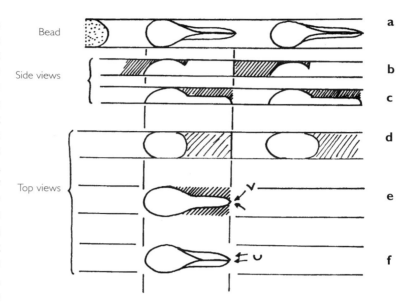

FIG 12.10 THE SEQUENCE OF CARVING THE TADPOLES FROM THE BEAD STARTS WITH (**a**) POSITIONING THE TADPOLES, LEAVING SPACES IN BETWEEN. IN THE SIDE VIEW AT (**b**) THE BACKGROUND SPACES BETWEEN TADPOLES IS REDUCED TO THE BOX SURFACE AND THE HEADS OF THE TADPOLES ARE SHAPED. AT (**c**) THE THICKNESS OF THE TAILS IS SET. A 'UNIT' OF TADPOLES THAT HAS NOW BEEN CREATED IS SHOWN IN THE TOP VIEW (**d**). IN (**e**) A V TOOL OUTLINES THE TAIL, AND THE BACKGROUND IS CLEARED AWAY DOWN TO THE BOX LEVEL. THE TAIL IS FINISHED IN (**f**) WITH A SMALL QUICK GOUGE, CARVING THE SIDES OF THE TAIL AND INTO THE BODY.

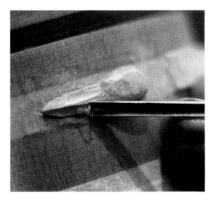

FIG 12.11 SHAPING THE TADPOLE TAILS WITH A SMALL QUICK GOUGE.

retained. The steps I took to carve the tadpoles are shown in Fig 12.10. Use a gouge upside down to cut the head shape, cleaning off wood to the thickness of the tails, which will need redrawing. Set in the tails with the V tool and shape them with a small quick gouge, going carefully to meet the background (see Fig 12.11).

Finishing

Use a small scraper and fine sandpaper to clean up and merge in the background, and the carving is complete. Check the work over in a different light and tidy up anything you have missed.

I used a very fine brush to apply a thin, water-based, green stain to the frog, leaf, join beads and the tadpoles, repeating this to build up a deeper colour in selected areas. You need to leave the sense of wood and grain, so put on less stain rather than more. When the wood is thoroughly dry, rub back the stained carving with the finest wire wool and finish the surface by hand with a light coat of sealer and beeswax. An old toothbrush is useful on the carved parts.

The holding spigot can now be removed from the box and its base flattened. I always leave the undersides of my boxes 'in the white', i.e. bare wood.

And that's the frog box and an example of carving in the round. As I said at the beginning, these techniques and approaches apply to any piece with a three-dimensional element, and will I hope be useful to you when you attempt your own designs.

Pierced relief I

CHAPTER 13

DOLPHIN MIRROR

I n several of the chapters in this book I have dealt with the different forms of relief carving; carving where the wood has been removed to varying depths from around the subject. The amount of wood that was removed from the background gave rise to low, medium or high relief. But what if some, or all of the background around a relief carving were removed altogether? This then becomes 'pierced relief'.

Pierced relief differs from 'work in the round' where wood is also removed from around the subject. In pierced relief the far more two-dimensional quality of the carving is maintained; the work should really only be viewed directly from the front, even if it is on a bowl that must be rotated. Although a carving or sculpture in the round often has a principal viewpoint (the one from which the work was originally conceived) it may have an infinite number of other viewpoints.

When work is pierced, the hole which is produced is framed by the remaining wood around it. In turn, the wood frames the remaining spaces. There is a dynamic between form and space. Although profiles are important in three-dimensional carving, which can be pierced in places, the spaces in a pierced relief must be given an equal importance to the wood that remains.

In the dolphin mirror project, which I am using to illustrate these points as well as more general techniques, you will see that I pay particular attention to making those lines where the space and form meet work as much as those within the form itself (see Figs 13.1 and 13.2). Let us look at this and other aspects of the design a bit closer.

INTRODUCTION

FIG 13.1 THE DOLPHIN MIRROR – REAL SKY!

DESIGN

The dolphin subject is contained within a turned frame, which is the starting point of the design. Mirror frames are bread and butter for many turners, but the difference here is that instead of opening up the whole face of the frame to reveal the mirror in its rebate, some of the wood is left to create the design.

You should also bear in mind that in flat pierced relief *you can see through the holes.* This might seem like an obvious point to make, but you should always be aware that the finished work will almost certainly be hung on a wall, which in effect fills in the pierced background, so for the correct effect you may find you have to repaper the living room! Consequently, the mirror is extremely effective here in hiding the wall, as well as simulating a watery background. When it comes to piercing three-dimensional forms such as bowls, the holes look in on themselves and so this problem does not arise.

FIG 13.2 THE ORIGINAL DRAWING FOR THE DOLPHIN MIRROR, 16IN (406MM) IN DIAMETER, SHOWING THE SIMPLE FLOWING LINES WHICH GIVE THE CARVING ITS EFFECT.

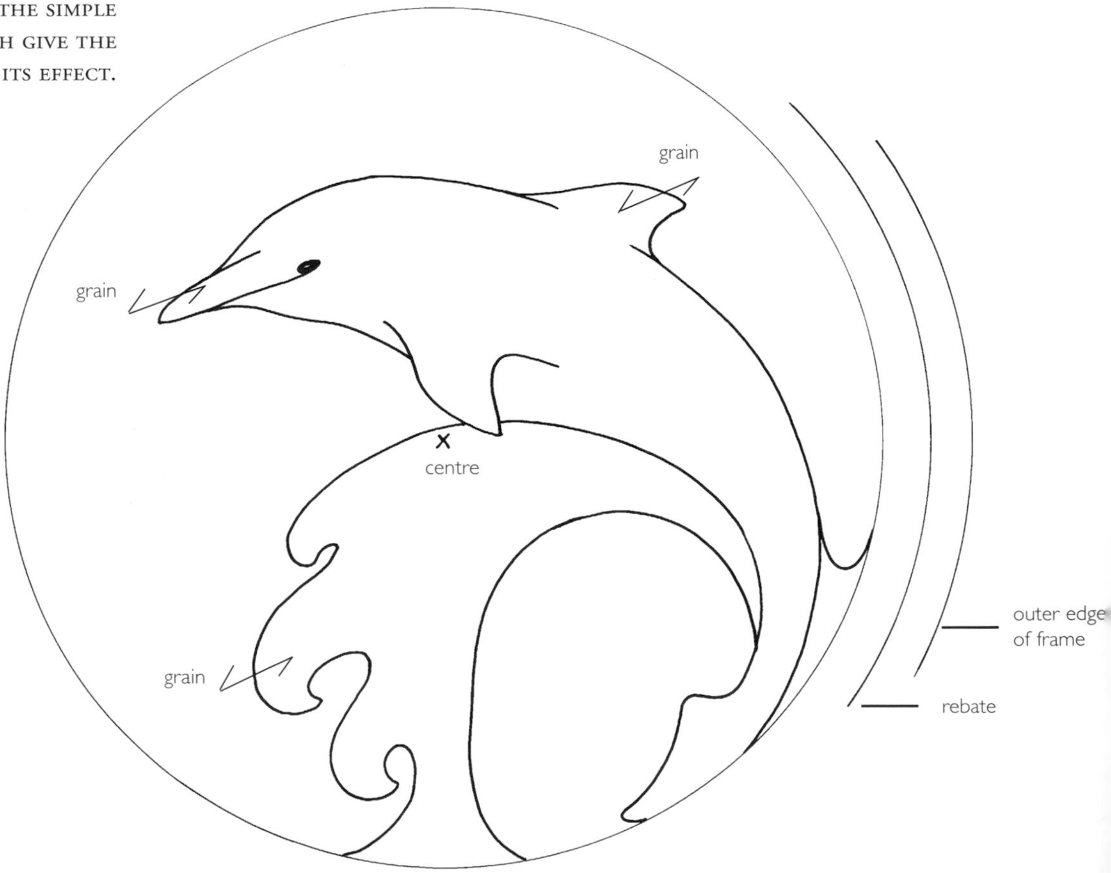

When the background is entirely removed from *any* carving, the piece becomes substantially weaker, and what strength remains depends in part on the thickness of the remaining wood as well as the way the wood is supported, and the grain distributed in the design. In this project the wood remains fairly thick and retains some strength because of that thickness. By contrast the ivy-leaf plate in Chapter 14 has less wood removed but what remains is substantially thinner. On balance the removal of wood necessitates a similar amount of care in the carving of both pieces. When the dolphin mirror is finished, much of the weakness is countered by the supporting effect of the mirror. So, remember that the work gets unnervingly weaker when it is pierced and, if you attempt this project, beware – it is not for faint hearts. Do take it in a relaxed and careful manner.

I continued the circular rhythm of the frame into the shape of the dolphin, giving it the sense of flow and movement for which dolphins are famous. As in other work in this book the waves and the dolphin are 'stylized' – meaning I used a degree of artistic licence to get the effect I wanted, while leaving enough of the mirror visible to be used *as* a mirror. Of course, you could use a different wood as a contrasting background instead of a mirror.

I kept the frame part of the work fairly small but made the whole thing as big as my lathe could take. The mirror was bought from a DIY superstore, where a large range of sizes is usually available. Mirror bevels are not a problem – the mirror I used had one, and it was hidden by the rebate (see Fig 13.3).

In pierced relief carving you need to tie the weak parts of the design to the stronger parts and run long grain through the weaker elements. If you look at Fig 13.2 you will see that I have aligned the grain of the wood so that it lies along what would otherwise be weak elements: the beak of the dolphin and the dorsal fin. I also deliberately adjusted the design to maximize strength, by introducing the wave to support the body of the dolphin, and tying it to the frame. The idea is to try to give the impression of delicacy while actually maintaining as much strength as possible. Some undercutting also helps the effect. The end product is still fairly vulnerable and must always be placed out of the reach of children – and adults who like to test how strong things are!

Project: Dolphin mirror

Turning

I used a tight-grained Japanese oak for this project; you need to choose a wood with a close, tight grain and delicate figuring. Woods such as beech, lime, sycamore, or cherry would also be suitable. The design was simple without much detail, but I needed to join it up to get the size I wanted. If you have to do this, it is very important to *make your joins good all the way along.* You will be removing material from parts of the joint which would normally compensate for any weakness elsewhere, and the last thing you want is a bad joint springing open.

The turning itself is basic faceplate work. The trick is to have a faceplate *smaller* than the mirror. Transfer the drawing to the bandsawn wood using carbon paper. Fix the faceplate on to the front by screwing through waste parts, and turn the recess which takes the mirror. Then reverse the work and fix it to the same faceplate – which now sits inside the recess – *using the same screw holes.* You must use screws that are of a length not to project from the hole on the other side.

Now turn the edge. I used a bowl gouge, a skew (as a scraper) for the beads and a spindle gouge for the cove between the beads.

Probably the most difficult procedure is turning the recess for the mirror, flat, *across the whole width of the wood.* You must make this flat or the mirror will not sit flush to the back of the carving. I used a sharp bowl gouge for this together with a straight edge, tidying the corners with a square scraper (see Fig 13.4).

The circular frame itself can be fully finished on the lathe. Note

FIG 13.3 SECTION THROUGH THE FRAME, SHOWING THE REBATE.

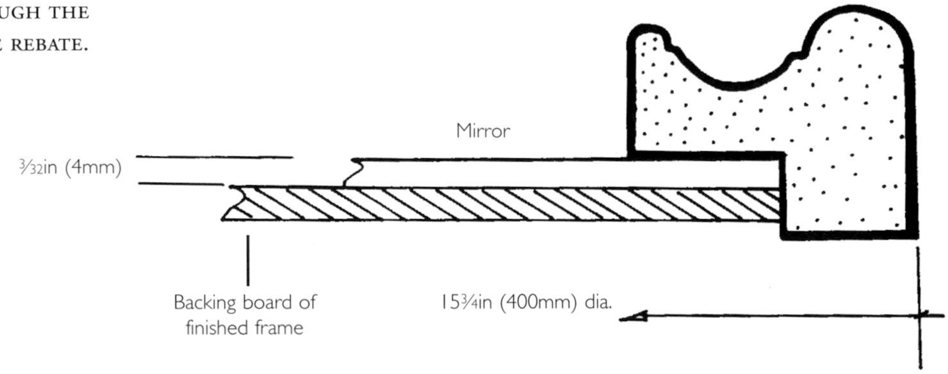

Mirror

³⁄₃₂in (4mm)

Backing board of
finished frame

15¾in (400mm) dia.

FIG 13.4 TURNING THE RECESS FOR THE MIRROR. IT IS IMPORTANT THAT THE SCREWS FOR THE FACEPLATE RESIDE BENEATH THE LEVEL TO WHICH WOOD IS REMOVED.

that the inner bead of the frame is given a groove which helps when the inside rim is shaped and wood is cut out around the dolphin.

Before removing the piece from the lathe, turn a backing plate the same diameter as the mirror. This will sit in the mirror recess during the boring and carving, supporting the increasingly delicate wood. I used 1in (25mm) MDF, but substantial plywood will do.

Piercing

The next stage is to bore the holes which will take the saw blade when cutting away the waste around the subject (see Fig 13.5). I used a pillar drill and Forstner bits to give me clean holes at right angles to the wood. Bore the holes, as many as you like, quite large *with the backing plate in position*, thus preventing the grain tearing as the bit exits on the other side.

FIG 13.5 HOLES BORED – 'PIERCED' – READY FOR SAWING. NOTE THAT WHEN THE DRAWING WAS TRANSFERRED TO THE WOODEN BLANK, IT LINED UP WITH THE GRAIN FOR STRENGTH.

Try to bore the holes at the following places:

- At weak junction points, where sawing might be too stressful on the wood.
- Where the saw would find a corner too tight to negotiate or turn in.
- Close to a line, serving as a right angled guide to the direction of the saw cuts.
- Accurately following a curved line in the design, which therefore might not need cleaning up further.

I removed the waste wood with a jigsaw (see Fig 13.6), but you can use a handsaw such as a coping or bow saw, in which case make sure it is well tensioned and the blade is not twisted.

When you saw it is very important to support the wood at all times. Work on the weaker parts first while they are strengthened by the other parts. Cut at right angles to the surface and keep as close to the line as you comfortably dare, resulting in less cleaning up. When piercing is complete, the work will be weak and flexible. From now on you must be careful to support any part of the carving on which you are putting pressure.

Carving and shaping tools

There are two stages to the carving. The first is cleaning up the frame, which is more properly 'shaping' (see Chapter 15) for which rasps and files are needed. The second stage is carving the dolphin and the waves using normal carving tools and methods. The main tools I used for the project were:

No. 8 x ⅛in (3mm).
Nos 4, 8 and V tool x ¼in (6mm).
Nos 4 and 8 x ½in (13mm).

All the tools were straight.

You may find you need different tools according to the detail and modelling you wish to include.

Carving

The first step is to clean up the frame. The frame's natural flexibility is not something to be afraid of, as it can also represent strength. Grip the frame in a bench vice and steady it with your body, but only work on that part which is supported in the vice. Use rasps and files to clean up the inner edge of the frame, taking care to follow the groove of the inner bead that was set in the preliminary turning (see Fig 13.7). You should be able to produce a clean circle that is indistinguishable from one turned on a lathe. Sand this inner edge to a finish.

Now the turned frame is complete, move on to the dolphin and waves. I used pieces of double-sided sticky tape to anchor the carving to its backing plate – not too much or separation will be difficult –

FIG 13.7 AFTER THE PIERCING IS FINISHED, A FILE IS USED, WITH THE GRAIN, TO FOLLOW THE LINE OF THE INNER EDGE OF THE FRAME.

FIG 13.8 THE FRAME PROPER IS COMPLETED AND THE WORK STUCK TO THE BACKING BOARD WITH DOUBLE-SIDED TAPE.

just around the edges of the pierced design (see Fig 13.8). This supports the work well enough for a small mallet to be used – with care! The plate itself can be clamped or screwed (countersink the heads) to the bench.

The carving is similar to that in previous chapters on unpierced relief work, except that the background has been cunningly removed to save a lot of work. There is enough wood in the dolphin to lose a lot of the flatness, rounding the body well and channelling the waves. A fair amount of modelling is possible too, although do

FIG 13.9 STARTING TO MODEL THE SURFACE. NOTE THE IMPROVISED CLAMP.

FIG 13.10 PARTING THE WAVES FROM THE DOLPHIN WITH THE V TOOL.

FIG 13.9

FIG 13.10

remember that this design is essentially a simple one (see Figs 13.9, 13.10, 13.11 and 13.12). When carving this piece, do bear in mind the following points.

When undercutting, be very careful not to split wood out from the opposite side. Use a slicing action with the grain and allow the edge to pass cleanly straight into the backing plate (see Fig 13.13). If you find the grain tearing out on the opposite side, stop short – there will be a chance to clean up when you reverse the carving later.

The undercutting needs to be selective; for example just the dorsal fin, the end of the tail and the lower edge of the waves.

Pay attention to the edges and get the lines clean and flowing. Use the maximum depth you have available; for example in the way the waves emerge from the side of the dolphin's tail. There is a gusset that links the tail to the frame, which can be taken back too.

With sharp tools you will not need to sandpaper the surface. Use a firmer chisel on the convex surfaces to pare finer and finer shavings. If you prefer a sanded finish, still use the tools as far as possible, as this will give a better and quicker result.

When the carving is complete, carefully lift the mirror frame from the fixing tape with a tool such as a spatula. You will see the carving is even weaker now, and remains delicate until the mirror is in position. Turn the carving over on the flat bench and hold it with five or six nails, set at intervals around the outside edge. Using light cuts, clean up the edges and emphasize any undercutting, for

FIG 13.11 MODELLING THE DOLPHIN IN RELATION TO THE WAVES. MAKE FULL USE OF THE DEPTH AVAILABLE.

FIG 13.12 THE EYE IS SET IN WITH A SMALL NUMBER 8 GOUGE.

FIG 13.11

FIG 13.12

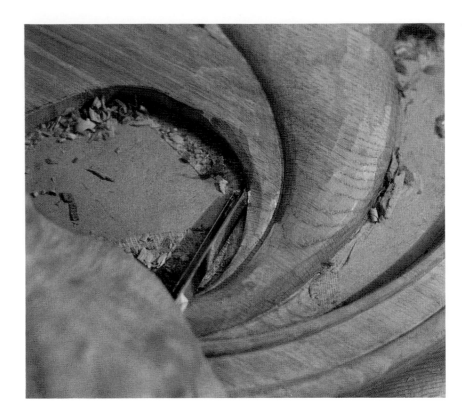

FIG 13.13 ONE WAY OF
UNDERCUTTING THE WAVES
IS WITH THE V TOOL, WORKING
WITH THE GRAIN AND CUTTING
SIMULTANEOUSLY INTO THE
BACKING PLATE.

FIG 13.14 AFTER THE FRONT IS
FINISHED, THE CARVING IS REVERSED
AND THE BACK UNDERCUTTING
EMPHASIZED AND CLEANED UP, THE
NAILS HOLDING THE WORK STILL FOR
CARVING.

example, under the tail (see Fig 13.14). You can use fine sandpaper along all the very edges to soften them *slightly*.

Finishing

The carving is now complete. Clean off the backing plate which you used earlier and put the frame back on – this will support the wood against the pressures of waxing and other finishing processes. I chose to use a liming paste on the dolphin – again artistic licence – which was then lightly buffed over with very fine sandpaper to reveal the soft tool marks, giving movement and direction to the surface form. I never use wire wool on oak. The whole piece was then dressed with a couple of coats of pale beeswax and buffed.

The mirror is held in position with a cover of hardboard, pinned like a picture frame, and the cover itself has a hanging ring.

Pierced relief II

CHAPTER 14

IVY-LEAF PLATE

The pierced relief I carved in Chapter 13 – the dolphin mirror – was fairly bulky; there was a lot of wood left even though a lot had been removed. The shapes were fairly large and I was able to support the carving from behind with a backing plate.

However, the wood could have been thinner, the grain unable to fall in the most propitious direction, or the design awkward to get at. In such cases techniques have to be adapted, new techniques introduced, or things done in a different order to achieve a satisfactory result. The project in this chapter brings up several new problems, which require this adaptable approach, and demonstrates

INTRODUCTION

FIG 14.1 THE IVY-LEAF
PLATE IN SYCAMORE.

some more characteristics of pierced carving, including more variable undercutting and a different way of holding the tools.

The ivy-leaf plate has a more decorative function than utilitarian, though it may still be used to display some cheesy comestible (see Fig 14.1). Certain features of the design are worth exploring a little.

DESIGN I looked at a lot of ivy in the garden to get a sense of the way the leaves hang in a regular pattern, and their basic forms. I also referred to some gardening books as part of my research, and here found that ivy is an extremely varied plant which I thought might bear further research for use as a decorative device in the future. If you decide to do this project, please bear in mind that my version of ivy is only one of many possible variations and by all means use different varieties and layouts if you prefer them. The plate was essentially flat, sweeping up at the edge. There is scope here for turning a different profile on which to work, for example, something more bowl-like, or for creating a series of turned vessels with a carved theme.

After I had an idea of what ivy leaves were like, I tried to achieve interest and variation by balancing the amount of pierced carving with the empty space making up the rest of the plate. The eye would soon get bored if the plate was decorated uniformly. This is a good principle for turning as well – many a table leg is overworked, and many a design has too much detail. Always try to keep things simple.

I put the design near the edge of the plate for the same reason of creating interest through variation, and also for interest through unpredictability (see Fig 14.2). The leaves break up the outline of the plate along a proportion of the edge, although the very tips still follow a sort of 'virtual edge'. Ivy has this sort of invasive image, breaking up the outline of trees and walls, and this helps to set a mood here as well. The edge of the plate remaining *within* the leaf design I made jagged, suggesting an echo of other leaves not included.

Next you need to decide on the shape, size and placing of the leaves. In the garden, the leaves by and large seemed to orientate in the same direction – ivy would appear to be quite an ordered plant, though it does not have that reputation – so I kept to a regular alignment or pattern of leaves. You could try a more random, less ordered approach, which of course would produce a completely different effect.

I chose not to put in the stalks. They seemed to complicate

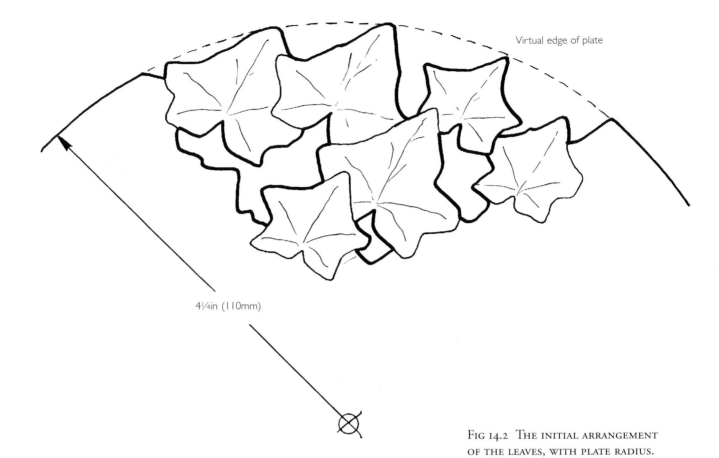

Virtual edge of plate

4¼in (110mm)

FIG 14.2 THE INITIAL ARRANGEMENT
OF THE LEAVES, WITH PLATE RADIUS.

matters and as I've said in previous chapters, I am not trying to imitate life, but to give a stylized impression of it. In practical terms the stalks would have been weak and vulnerable in a pierced state, and the plate was in any case quite thin to start with. The stalks could be managed better if the work, or the stalk part of the work, was a non-pierced, low relief carving. If you do decide to include them, you will need to maximize the strength of the grain by running it along the stalks, or tying a stalk to some other element of the design.

The design of leaves was worked out on bits of tracing paper first, shuffling individual leaves around until a pleasing arrangement was achieved. I set the leaves *across* the grain, although it was a toss up as to which way was best. Strong grain one way was weak in another. Putting aside the pierced nature of the background, the remaining wood is essentially a flat, low relief carving, with little depth available for modelling. Fig 14.3 shows the spaces-to-be blackened for clarity.

FIG 14.3 THE DESIGN WAS TRACED ON THE WOOD. FOR CLARITY THE AREAS WHICH MUST BE PIERCED ARE BLOCKED IN BLACK.

Project: Ivy-leaf plate

Turning

The plate is a normal piece of faceplate turning, using a dovetail collet chuck in a recess at the back to hold the work (see Fig 14.4). Most of the plate is flat, rising towards the edges, and the centre section is thicker than the edges, which has a bearing on the amount of undercutting.

'Undercutting' means exactly that: wood is removed from beneath a part of the carving in order to throw it into higher relief and to make it appear more delicate. Towards the edge of the plate, where the wood is thinner, there is less need to undercut to get the lightness of effect. This will become more evident later in the project, but it is worth bearing in mind at this stage.

The wood I used was a bit of air-dried sycamore. I chose it because it had started to show signs of 'foxing' (darker streaks and discolorations from fungus infestations). This slightly decaying look seemed to suit the ivy theme, but did make the wood a little 'woollier' than I would have liked. Obviously for delicate work your material must be sound and close-grained.

I sanded the plate to a fine finish. This goes against my rule of carving only unsanded wood to save damage to the cutting edges,

and means that for the final cuts, after the sanded wood has been removed, you must definitely check the cutting edges of your tools.

It is practically impossible to carve the plate on the lathe, so it must come off and on to your bench. I still used the lathe chuck though, held in a vice with a pair of gripping blocks (see Figs 14.5 and 14.6). Later on I needed to take the plate off the chuck in order to get to the centre section. Clamping across the middle was then the option. Note the adjustable vice that I am using in Fig 14.5 – this

FIG 14.5 THE CHUCK GRIPPED IN
BLOCKS OF WOOD. THESE COULD BE
HELD IN AN ORDINARY BENCH VICE,
BUT GREATER CONTROL AND ACCESS IS
POSSIBLE WITH AN ADJUSTABLE
SWIVEL BALL CLAMP. THIS ONE IS
MADE BY KOCH. THE EXCELLENT
FRANKLIN SPENCER HYDRACLAMP IS
AN ALTERNATIVE.

FIG 14.6 TWO BLOCKS OF WOOD
WERE USED TO GRIP THE CIRCULAR
CROSS-SECTION OF THE CHUCK IN
THE VICE.

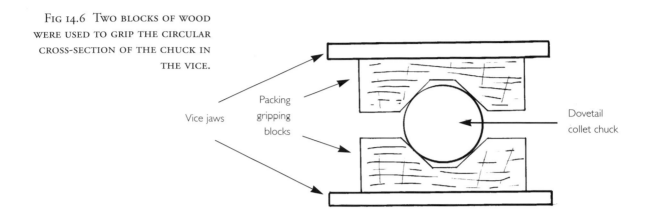

Vice jaws

Packing
gripping
blocks

Dovetail
collet chuck

one is made by Koch and really makes the job much easier. If you
are carving or otherwise working away from the lathe, I strongly
recommend you investigate using an adjustable, swivel ball holding
device.

Piercing

I worked on the outer leaves first, keeping the strength of the inner
wood until it was pierced later, but how you approach this will
depend on your design.

With the plate held firmly in position, the first stage is to bore
holes to take the saw blade which frets out the waste. For the sawing
I used a small fret saw with a fine blade for the wood towards the
edge – the thinnest – and a coping saw for the thicker wood towards
the centre. The required holes can be quite small, and because the
rim is thin and delicate, small holes are less traumatic on the wood.

To be extra-careful, I used a wheel brace, as I didn't want the wood
splitting out as the bit came through. Do make sure your drill bit is
sharp.

Fret saws and coping saws have detachable blades, threaded
through the holes and reassembled. Make sure the blade is not
twisted, and is tense without being overtense; in this way there is less
likelihood of damaging the blade (see Fig 14.7).

You must support the wood with the fingers of one hand as you saw
through. You will find the wood starts to flex quite soon but go *with*
the flexing; it is surprising the amount of movement you can get away
with. Come as close to the line as possible and if you feel confident
enough, tilt the saw so as to start some measure of undercutting.

Carving tools

For the ivy plate carving the main tools I used were:

No. 9 x ⅛in (3mm).
Nos 3, 5 and V tool x ¼in (6mm).
Skew chisel x ⅜in (10mm).

Carving

When the first area of piercing is complete, you can start cleaning up the edges with the carving tools. A small amount of surface modelling is possible but the main effect is in the piercing and setting of one leaf against another.

Although the surface flexes, sharp tools will still cut it. However, you will need to adjust the way you hold your carving tools so that the fingers of the blade hand can take on a supporting role, bracing the wood against the cut of the edge.

Look at Fig 14.8 carefully and you will see the trick of bringing the thumb of the blade hand across and against the metal, while the remaining fingers curl around the wood. This is a common whittling (knife) technique and allows you to pare away the material safely – all fingers and thumb are behind the cutting edge, even if some of

FIG 14.7 FRETTING THE EDGE: NOTE THE BORE HOLES TO TAKE THE BLADE. MY OTHER HAND IS WORKING THE CAMERA, BUT WOULD NORMALLY BE SUPPORTING THE WOOD FROM BEHIND.

FIG 14.8 SEPARATING THE LEAVES WITH A V TOOL: NOTE THE WAY THE TOOL IS BEING HELD AND MANIPULATED.

FIG 14.9 RELIEVING ONE LEAF FROM THE NEXT WITH A FLAT GOUGE.

FIG 14.10 FRETTING THE INNER ROW OF HOLES. I DO THE FRETTING IN STAGES TO MAKE THE MOST OF THE MATERIAL STRENGTH.

them are behind the wood as well. Be sure to keep the fingers out of the way at all times, and especially when the edge is coming out of the wood.

The low relief carving proceeds as elsewhere in this book. The V tool is used to chase the profile of a leaf, then the background (which is a leaf behind) is cut away with the flat number 3 gouge (see Fig 14.9). The cutting edges of various gouges, including the small

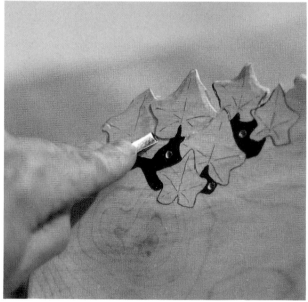

FIG 14.9

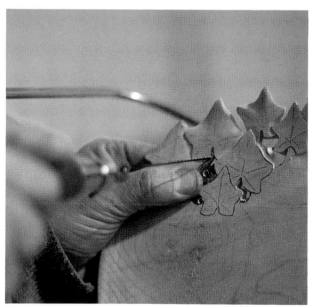

FIG 14.10

number 9, can also be used to set in edges that cannot be negotiated with the V tool.

When the outermost, more delicate, leaves have been finished from the viewing position, turn to the back of the plate and chamfer the edges cleanly. Mitre and join any corners neatly. Do not undercut so as to make the edge too thin; about 45° should be enough.

Repeat the piercing, fretting and carving as before to the inner parts (see Figs 14.10 and 14.11). You will find that these parts become thicker towards the centre of the plate (unless you have made the plate uniformly thin). This means that you must undercut more radically. You can use the same method to hold the gouges as you did when carving the front, supporting the wood from behind with the blade fingers, and using the thumb to control the cut of the gouge (see Fig 14.12). If your gouges are at their sharpest then fairly strong cuts can be taken quite safely. I removed the plate from the chuck to make getting at the back easier.

Pay attention to getting the edges crisp, and alter the light now and then to get a clean surface. You may need to enlist the help of a fine knife, a riffler, or a small needle file. The veins of the ivy can be chased in with the V tool (see Fig 14.13). In this deeper section of wood more modelling is possible, including some undercutting between the leaves.

I chose to sand the surfaces of the leaves smooth in keeping with

FIG 14.11 PIERCING IS COMPLETE, AND THE LEAVES ARE NOW QUITE FLEXIBLE.

FIG 14.12 THE NARROW EDGE NEEDS ONLY LIGHT UNDERCUTTING BUT TOWARDS THE CENTRE OF THE PLATE, HEAVIER CUTS ARE REQUIRED.

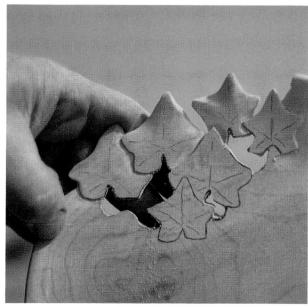

FIG 14.11

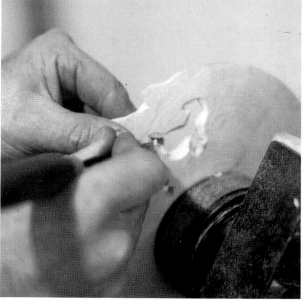

FIG 14.12

FIG 14.13 CHASING IN THE VEINS
WITH A V TOOL.

the rest of the plate when the carving was finished. Make sure the very edges are clean and finish off with at least 240 grit, going along the grain.

Finishing

The plate was given several thin coats of beeswax, very lightly coloured to put some 'body' into the wood. I found the natural whiteness of the sycamore just a bit too bland, and the colour brought some figuring and foxiness to the piece. You could also give the plate a walnut oil finish, which is suitable for finishing pieces which may be used for serving food.

Shaping

CHAPTER 15

PESTLE AND MORTAR

I n the introductory chapter of this book I made a distinction
between 'carving' and 'shaping' wood. I implied that for a
workpiece to be called 'carved' there must be a use of traditional
carving tools and methods of cutting and working, which produces
a particular carved look as the end result. Shaping on the other hand
can be seen as the use of rasps, files and sandpaper and often relying
heavily on the beauty of the wood in the final result, with a softer,
more modelled appearance.

Without making competitive comparisons, this distinction is
useful in helping students be clear as to which approach they wish to
take. A student may get confused in the world of carving when all
the while he or she only wants to do some simple shaping. Carving

INTRODUCTION

FIG 15.1 THE FINISHED PESTLE AND
MORTAR IN YEW WOOD. IF THE PESTLE
IS SWUNG AROUND ITS HANDLE WILL
BE FOUND TO BE A SIZE THAT WILL FIT
SNUGLY INTO THE HOLLOW OF THE
LIP.

gouges are not what they want at all, and to keep referring to 'wanting to do a bit of carving' is not helpful. So I make this distinction seriously, but mainly for didactic reasons. There are areas of work, and occasions, when the two approaches overlap.

In this chapter I will be looking at a pestle and mortar – or more particularly the mortar (see Fig 15.1), and especially the pouring spout of the mortar. This feature can be a very beautiful touch to *any* bowl from which something may be poured. Although it certainly helps when pouring liquids, powdered spices and grains can also be poured accurately from the lip. As I mentioned in Chapter 5 this sort of woodware comes under the heading of 'treen' – domestic, mainly country, pieces used in the past by those who could not afford pewter.

While I have tried to make the mortar as attractive as possible, I am keen on any object which *looks* as if it has a function being able to *perform* it, not just to look decorative.

To create the simple shape of the lip it is best to use rasps and files to get the shapes you want. This will give you an opportunity to look at how these tools are used to shape wood. But first let us consider the design.

DESIGN If this mortar were made by a potter, the bowl would be thrown from clay to the finished shape on what is, to all intents and purposes, a horizontal faceplate. A potter would apply a finger and thumb to the edge and squeeze out the lip into the shape required. This seems to epitomize the difference between modelling (which builds up a pliable shape), and crafts which use a reductive process (removing material from a larger, fixed shape). The latter would include both turning and carving. I am sure that many woodturners have wished they could just give their bowl a 'little squeeze' to get the right shape!

The problem for us 'reductionists' is to create the lip in the bowl from oversized wood. As the wood spins about the axis of the lathe, an amount must be left where the lip will be. The axial rotation means wood is left all around the circumference, or not at all. The profile of the lip becomes a profiled ridge around the whole vessel (see Fig 15.2). After turning, most of the excess lip profile must be carved away to that of the mortar bowl proper and the lip and bowl merged so that the lip looks like a natural outpouring of the edge.

The mortar itself must be strong, and the pestle comfortable to work in the palm of your hand. As the lip is a feature – in fact the most interesting feature in what is otherwise a very simple shape – the design is generous, but you can always make the lip smaller if you wish. One feature of this project that is not immediately evident is that the handle of the pestle sits snugly in the lip of the mortar when not in use.

For the mortar I used a tough, tight-grained piece of yew. The wood must obviously be as hard as possible, but to some extent the hardness required depends on what level of grinding is intended. Yew, maple, and beechwood are fine for most work and versions of the pestle and mortar that I have made using yew continue to give excellent service after many years. Heavy pounding needs something like boxwood, though you may have problems getting the size, or even lignum if you can find an old bowls ball.

For the pestle I combined a yew handle with a boxwood grinding face, mainly for the contrast. A single piece of hard yew would have worked just as well I'm sure.

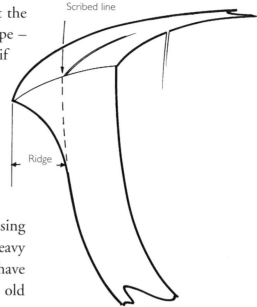

FIG 15.2 SECTION THROUGH THE LIP OF THE MORTAR. THE SIZE AND SHAPE OF THE LIP IS OF COURSE A PERSONAL CHOICE.

Project: Pestle and mortar

Turning

The mortar is essentially a hollow vessel with a thick, strong wall, and as such is a fairly straightforward piece of turning (see Fig 15.3). Again, I tend to make the base a little thicker. Remember that when the outside is turned, the profile of the lip must be left as a ridge around the edge. The outside wall can be sanded to a finish right up to this ridge.

Reversed, the inside is simply hollowed out. Again the inside can be properly finished, as can the uppermost edge of the bowl, and the ridge.

Before turning off the lathe use the long point of a skew chisel, or a scribe, and mark a line around the edge to the thickness of the wall (see Fig 15.4). You can eye the line from the outside curve of the bowl, or measure it. The line is the finished edge of the mortar

FIG 15.3 HOLLOWING THE MORTAR WITH A ROUGHING GOUGE. THE RIDGE FROM WHICH THE LIP WILL BE SHAPED IS CLEARLY VISIBLE.

behind the lip, and you must work accurately to this line. Don't score it deeply, just enough to be clearly visible.

Shaping

After the bowl has been turned the next stage is to mark out the position and shape of the lip, making sure the grain runs into it for maximum strength (see Fig 15.5). Mark where the lip comes on the underside of the ridge as well.

By tilting the table on a bandsaw to line up with the side of the mortar you can remove most of the ridge, leaving waste around the lip – this is why the position was marked previously on the underside (see Fig 15.6). If you do not have a bandsaw, a standard coping saw will do the trick, holding the mortar in a vice.

Because the bowl of the mortar is strong and thick it can be

FIG 15.4 SCRIBING THE LINE WHICH WILL BE THE SHAPED EDGE, EXCEPT FOR THE LIP.

FIG 15.5 THE SYMMETRICAL LIP
DRAWN IN. FOR CLARITY I HAVE
BLACKED OUT SOME OF THE WOOD
WHICH NEEDS TO BE REMOVED.

gripped in a vice from edge to base, and probably across as well. If
the jaws of the vice are lined, there is no danger of marking the
vessel. Later when you want to shape the inside of the lip – where it
forms the spout – you can bridge across with clamps as was done
with the lettered bowl in Chapter 6.

Remember that rasps and files are the principal means of shaping
wood. Rasps have individual teeth and cut more, or less, coarsely;
files have ridges across the metal and will give very fine cuts. As files
are designed for metal they tend to clog when used on wood, so
regular wire brushing is required, likewise with the rasps. 'Rifflers'
are widely available; these are smaller paddle-shaped rasps in a
variety of useful shapes. Perhaps the best rasps and rifflers that I
know of are made by Auriou – each tooth is individually cut by
hand. Two important points need to be borne in mind when

FIG 15.6 BANDSAWING AWAY MOST OF
THE RIDGE WITH THE TABLE TILTED.
REMEMBER TO STOP SHORT OF WHERE
THE LIP STARTS.

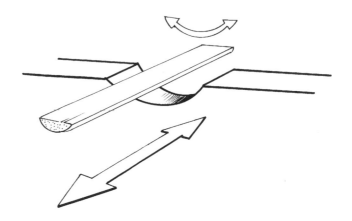

FIG 15.7 TO GET THE BEST CUT FROM
A RASP OR FILE, A SIDEWAYS SWEEP
COMBINED WITH THE FORWARD
MOTION IS NEEDED. ALWAYS WORK
WITH THE GRAIN WHERE POSSIBLE.

working with rasps, files and rifflers:

- To use rasps effectively, files or rifflers, you must combine a sideways drift as the tool moves backwards and forwards (see Figs 15.7 and 15.8). This prevents grooves and ridges forming.
- Always work *with* the grain and try to sweep the rasp, file or riffler smoothly around the curve you are visualizing (see Fig 15.9). Try not to leave 'flats'.

These points apply to all rasps, files and rifflers, no matter what their size.

Start the shaping by working the curved sides of the bowl smoothly to the scribed line of the edge. You want to get an exact look, as if it were actually turned, for the best effect. Remember the two points above and work with the grain to get a surface which only

FIG 15.8 THE STARTING POSITION FOR
THE RASP . . .

. . . WHICH FINISHES UP FORWARDS
AND SWEPT TO THE SIDE GIVING A
CLEAN CUT.

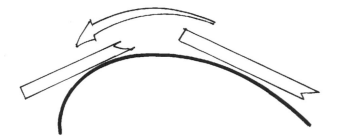
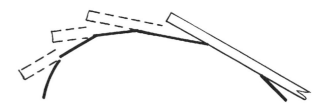

needs a light amount of sanding to finish.

When you get to the lip itself you may like to change briefly back to a flat carving tool for removing wood towards the point (see Fig 15.10), returning to the rasps and files for smoothing.

If you look carefully at Fig 15.11 you can see that I have created three planes around the lip: one coming in from either side, and a third plane curving up from beneath. This helps to make more of a feature of the lip, but the fact is that the plane coming from beneath is the only surface remaining from the original turning. If you wish you can smooth all this out and give the rounded effect that a potter might give to clay. Personally I don't like this modelled look as much as I do those sharper changes of plane which are more truly a characteristic of carving and shaping.

You can now sand the outer surface smooth and turn your

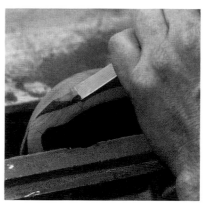

FIG 15.10 A FEW STROKES WITH A CARVING TOOL TO START OFF THE LIP SHAPE.

FIG 15.11 CLOSE-UP OF THE LIP SHOWING THE DISTINCT CHANGES IN PLANE THAT ARE VERY MUCH A FEATURE OF CARVED WORK, AS OPPOSED TO MODELLED WORK.

FIG 15.12 THE HOLDING BRIDGE. A
DEEP GOUGE CAN BE USED TO START
TO HOLLOW THE SPOUT-LIKE EFFECT
ON THE LIP.

attention to the channel that runs from the lip into the hollow of
the vessel. Fig 15.12 shows the holding bridge I made using two
battens and two quick action clamps. The thicker batten below is
held in a bench vice. I felt happier taking most of the holding
pressure in the centre packing, rather than the edges, but you will
have to use your own judgement on this.

A quick gouge will neatly start the channel and run it into the
hollow of the mortar. I followed the gouge with a riffler which
curves around the lip (see Fig 15.13). Flat abrasive tools will also do
the job. Finish with sandpaper wrapped around an appropriate
dowel. Fig 15.14 shows a close-up of the hollow inside the lip.
Notice that I have again left a distinct change of plane where the lip
meets the top edge of the bowl. Smooth away any trace of the

FIG 15.13 CHANGING TO A RIFFLER
FOR SHAPING.

FIG 15.14 CLOSE-UP OF THE HOLLOW
INSIDE THE LIP. DISTINCT CORNERS
CAN BE SEEN TO EITHER SIDE OF THE
HOLLOW, CONTRASTING WITH THE
OTHERWISE SMOOTH SHAPE, TO ADD
VARIETY AND INTEREST.

scribed line. You may choose to shape the channel so that it merges with the edge.

The mortar is now finished. Have a look at it in different lights to check the surface finish.

The pestle is made between centres. Turn two cylinders, one of beech with a spigot and one of boxwood with a matching hole and glue them together. I used pressure from the lathe centres as a clamp. When the glue is dry, it is simply a matter of shaping. Try to get the grinding edge something like the profile of the inside base of the bowl and you will find you can 'pestle' better.

Finishing

Both the pestle and mortar were finished with walnut oil.

Bibliography

Bütz, R. (1984) *How to Carve Wood.* Newtown, CT: Taunton Press.

Darlow, M. (1985) *The Practice of Woodturning.* Melaleuca Press.

Hasluck, P. (1911) *Manual of Traditional Woodcarving.* New York: Dover.

Norbury, I. (1987) *Relief Woodcarving and Lettering.* Newtown, CT: Stobart & Sons.

Pye, C. (1994) *Woodcarving Tools, Materials and Equipment.* Lewes: Guild of Master Craftsman Publications.

Roszkiewicz, R. (1984) *The Woodturners Companion.* New York: Sterling.

Small, T. and Woodbridge, C. (1987) *Mouldings and Turned Woodwork of the 16th, 17th and 18th Centuries.* London: Stobart & Sons.

Wheeler, W. and Hayward, C. (1963) *Practical Woodcarving and Gilding.* London: Evans.

Woodcarving magazine. Lewes: Guild of Master Craftsman Publications.

METRIC CONVERSION TABLE

INCHES TO MILLIMETRES AND CENTIMETRES
MM = MILLIMETRES CM = CENTIMETRES

INCHES	MM	CM	INCHES	CM	INCHES	CM
⅛	3	0.3	9	22.9	30	76.2
¼	6	0.6	10	25.4	31	78.7
⅜	10	1.0	11	27.9	32	81.3
½	13	1.3	12	30.5	33	83.8
⅝	16	1.6	13	33.0	34	86.4
¾	19	1.9	14	35.6	35	88.9
⅞	22	2.2	15	38.1	36	91.4
1	25	2.5	16	40.6	37	94.0
1¼	32	3.2	17	43.2	38	96.5
1½	38	3.8	18	45.7	39	99.1
1¾	44	4.4	19	48.3	40	101.6
2	51	5.1	20	50.8	41	104.1
2½	64	6.4	21	53.3	42	106.7
3	76	7.6	22	55.9	43	109.2
3½	89	8.9	23	58.4	44	111.8
4	102	10.2	24	61.0	45	114.3
4½	114	11.4	25	63.5	46	116.8
5	127	12.7	26	66.0	47	119.4
6	152	15.2	27	68.6	48	121.9
7	178	17.8	28	71.1	49	124.5
8	203	20.3	29	73.7	50	127.0

Index

About the author

C hris Pye has been both a professional woodcarver and woodturner for nearly 20 years, beginning with carving, which remains his first love. While carving on turned work some 15 years ago, he began to practice woodturning himself, and now feels at home in both crafts, often combining them.

His carved work, which is mainly commissioned, covers a broad spectrum, ranging from lettering to ornamental bedheads, figurework and personal sculpture, to the restoration of old carvings and decorative work on furniture.

His turned work, also commissioned, includes newel posts, stair parts and table legs for the trade, as well as individual bowls, boxes and one-off pieces. In 1991 he demonstrated at the Association of Woodturners of Great Britain's International Seminar in Loughborough.

Chris Pye has several years of experience teaching adult education classes in woodcarving, as well as private students in both turning and carving. He runs regular courses from his home near the Black Mountains on the Welsh border.

He contributes regularly to *Woodcarving* and *Woodturning* magazines, and his previous book, *Woodcarving Tools, Materials and Equipment* is becoming a standard reference work in the field. He is currently working on his next book, on letter carving.

Born in County Durham in 1952, Chris has been deeply involved with Buddhism since he was a teenager, and this is often reflected in his attitude to his work, writing and teaching. He is married with two sons, Daniel and Finian, and enjoys walking in the local mountains and kite flying.

Chris Pye
The Poplars
Ewyas Harold
Hereford HR2 0HU

GMC Publications
BOOKS

WOODCARVING

The Art of the Woodcarver	GMC Publications
Carving Architectural Detail in Wood: The Classical Tradition	
	Frederick Wilbur
Carving Birds & Beasts	GMC Publications
Carving Nature: Wildlife Studies in Wood	Frank Fox-Wilson
Carving Realistic Birds	David Tippey
Decorative Woodcarving	Jeremy Williams
Elements of Woodcarving	Chris Pye
Essential Tips for Woodcarvers	GMC Publications
Essential Woodcarving Techniques	Dick Onians
Further Useful Tips for Woodcarvers	GMC Publications
Lettercarving in Wood: A Practical Course	Chris Pye
Making & Using Working Drawings for Realistic Model Animals	
	Basil F. Fordham
Power Tools for Woodcarving	David Tippey
Practical Tips for Turners & Carvers	GMC Publications
Relief Carving in Wood: A Practical Introduction	Chris Pye
Understanding Woodcarving	GMC Publications
Understanding Woodcarving in the Round	GMC Publications
Useful Techniques for Woodcarvers	GMC Publications
Wildfowl Carving – Volume 1	Jim Pearce
Wildfowl Carving – Volume 2	Jim Pearce
Woodcarving: A Complete Course	Ron Butterfield
Woodcarving: A Foundation Course	Zoë Gertner
Woodcarving for Beginners	GMC Publications
Woodcarving Tools & Equipment Test Reports	GMC Publications
Woodcarving Tools, Materials & Equipment	Chris Pye

WOODTURNING

Adventures in Woodturning	David Springett
Bert Marsh: Woodturner	Bert Marsh
Bowl Turning Techniques Masterclass	Tony Boase
Colouring Techniques for Woodturners	Jan Sanders
Contemporary Turned Wood: New Perspectives in a Rich Tradition	
	Ray Leier, Jan Peters & Kevin Wallace
The Craftsman Woodturner	Peter Child
Decorative Techniques for Woodturners	Hilary Bowen
Fun at the Lathe	R.C. Bell
Further Useful Tips for Woodturners	GMC Publications
Illustrated Woodturning Techniques	John Hunnex
Intermediate Woodturning Projects	GMC Publications
Keith Rowley's Woodturning Projects	Keith Rowley
Practical Tips for Turners & Carvers	GMC Publications
Turning Green Wood	Michael O'Donnell
Turning Miniatures in Wood	John Sainsbury
Turning Pens and Pencils	Kip Christensen & Rex Burningham
Understanding Woodturning	Ann & Bob Phillips
Useful Techniques for Woodturners	GMC Publications
Useful Woodturning Projects	GMC Publications
Woodturning: Bowls, Platters, Hollow Forms, Vases, Vessels, Bottles, Flasks, Tankards, Plates	GMC Publications
Woodturning: A Foundation Course (New Edition)	Keith Rowley
Woodturning: A Fresh Approach	Robert Chapman
Woodturning: An Individual Approach	Dave Regester
Woodturning: A Source Book of Shapes	John Hunnex
Woodturning Jewellery	Hilary Bowen
Woodturning Masterclass	Tony Boase
Woodturning Techniques	GMC Publications
Woodturning Tools & Equipment Test Reports	GMC Publications
Woodturning Wizardry	David Springett

WOODWORKING

Bird Boxes and Feeders for the Garden	Dave Mackenzie
Complete Woodfinishing	Ian Hosker
David Charlesworth's Furniture-Making Techniques	
	David Charlesworth
Furniture & Cabinetmaking Projects	GMC Publications
Furniture-Making Projects for the Wood Craftsman	GMC Publications
Furniture-Making Techniques for the Wood Craftsman	GMC Publications
Furniture Projects	Rod Wales
Furniture Restoration (Practical Crafts)	Kevin Jan Bonner
Furniture Restoration and Repair for Beginners	Kevin Jan Bonner
Furniture Restoration Workshop	Kevin Jan Bonner
Green Woodwork	Mike Abbott
Kevin Ley's Furniture Projects	Kevin Ley
Making & Modifying Woodworking Tools	Jim Kingshott
Making Chairs and Tables	GMC Publications
Making Classic English Furniture	Paul Richardson
Making Little Boxes from Wood	John Bennett
Making Shaker Furniture	Barry Jackson
Making Woodwork Aids and Devices	Robert Wearing
Minidrill: Fifteen Projects	John Everett
Pine Furniture Projects for the Home	Dave Mackenzie
Practical Scrollsaw Patterns	John Everett
Router Magic: Jigs, Fixtures and Tricks to Unleash your Router's Full Potential	Bill Hylton
Routing for Beginners	Anthony Bailey
The Scrollsaw: Twenty Projects	John Everett
Sharpening: The Complete Guide	Jim Kingshott
Sharpening Pocket Reference Book	Jim Kingshott
Simple Scrollsaw Projects	GMC Publications
Space-Saving Furniture Projects	Dave Mackenzie
Stickmaking: A Complete Course	Andrew Jones & Clive George
Stickmaking Handbook	Andrew Jones & Clive George
Test Reports: The Router and Furniture & Cabinetmaking	
	GMC Publications
Veneering: A Complete Course	Ian Hosker
Woodfinishing Handbook (Practical Crafts)	Ian Hosker
Woodworking with the Router: Professional Router Techniques any Woodworker can Use	
	Bill Hylton & Fred Matlack
The Workshop	Jim Kingshott

UPHOLSTERY

The Upholsterer's Pocket Reference Book	David James
Upholstery: A Complete Course (Revised Edition)	David James
Upholstery Restoration	David James
Upholstery Techniques & Projects	David James
Upholstery Tips and Hints	David James

TOYMAKING

Designing & Making Wooden Toys	Terry Kelly
Fun to Make Wooden Toys & Games	Jeff & Jennie Loader
Restoring Rocking Horses	Clive Green & Anthony Dew
Scrollsaw Toy Projects	Ivor Carlyle
Scrollsaw Toys for All Ages	Ivor Carlyle
Wooden Toy Projects	GMC Publications

MAGAZINES

WOODTURNING • WOODCARVING
FURNITURE & CABINETMAKING
THE ROUTER • WOODWORKING
THE DOLLS' HOUSE MAGAZINE
WATER GARDENING
EXOTIC GARDENING
GARDEN CALENDAR
OUTDOOR PHOTOGRAPHY
BUSINESSMATTERS

The above represents a full list of all titles currently published or scheduled to be published.
All are available direct from the Publishers or through bookshops, newsagents and specialist retailers.
To place an order, or to obtain a complete catalogue, contact:

GMC Publications,
Castle Place, 166 High Street, Lewes, East
Sussex BN7 1XU, United Kingdom
Tel: 01273 488005 Fax: 01273 478606
E-mail: pubs@thegmcgroup.com
Orders by credit card are accepted